Small Group Dynamics
for Dynamic Group Leaders

SMALL GROUP DYNAMICS

FOR **DYNAMIC**

GROUP LEADERS

BILLIE DAVIS

ELM HILL

A Division of
HarperCollins Christian Publishing

www.elmhillbooks.com

Small Group Dynamics for Dynamic Group Leaders

Published in Nashville, Tennessee, by Elm Hill, an imprint of Thomas Nelson. Elm Hill and Thomas Nelson are registered trademarks of HarperCollins Christian Publishing, Inc.

Elm Hill titles may be purchased in bulk for educational, business, fund-raising, or sales promotional use. For information, please e-mail SpecialMarkets@ThomasNelson.com.

All Scripture quotations are taken from the Holy Bible, New International Version®, NIV®. Copyright © 1973, 1978, 1984, 2011 by Biblica, Inc.® Used by permission of Zondervan. All rights reserved worldwide. www.Zondervan. com. The "NIV" and "New International Version" are trademarks registered in the United States Patent and Trademark Office by Biblica, Inc.®

Book design by Dawn M. Brandon (dawn@ravensbrook.net).

Library of Congress Cataloging-in-Publication Data

Library of Congress Control Number: 2018941265

ISBN 978-1-595557278 (Paperback)
ISBN 978-1-595557537 (Hardbound)
ISBN 978-1-595557551 (eBook)

CONTENTS

FOREWORD

WE WERE CREATED FOR RELATIONSHIP. The image of God that imprints us, marred as it may be, still draws us in spiritual hunger toward our Creator. It also draws us into circles of human relationship that profoundly shape our lives—family connections, friendship networks, working relationships, and Jesus-centered fellowships. We thrive best in relationship, we grow best in relationship, and we heal best in relationship. That is by divine design.

We also *learn* best in relationship. While studying undergraduate aerospace engineering at the University of Minnesota, I had a favorite teacher whose lectures on fluid mechanics were riveting. He had an odd way of printing and writing cursive at the same time, and he could fill the chalkboards faster than I could take notes. It just flowed out of him. He seemed to lose himself in wonder as he would lay out elegant equations and proofs and explanations. His lectures instilled in me a passion for a field that most people wanted to avoid.

But that experience, valuable as it was, centered on the old model of learning without relationship. That all changed when I entered graduate school and he became my advisor and I his research assistant. He walked me all the way through a Master's degree and a Ph.D. We spent five years together, solving problems, building experimental equipment, and publishing research. In somewhat Christian terms, I had gone from being a *student* to being a *disciple*. The difference? Relationship.

Add *relationship* to any group and you get, in the words of Billie Davis, a dynamic group. Her book is fittingly titled, for here she shows herself to be truly ahead of her time. When so many are still thinking education, she is thinking formation. Where many of us are still stuck in lecture/sermon paradigms, she is describing a model of spiritual formation that binds the learning experience to the dynamic of personal interaction. We really do learn best in the context of relationship.

Few people have influenced the scope and shape of Christian education in the Assemblies of God more than Billie Davis. Her passion is contagious, and her insights into group dynamics are invaluable to true learning. From sitting in a little red chair as a young girl in Sunday School to teaching in the university classroom, Billie Davis lives and exudes Christ's call for His people to learn and grow. Whatever the age of your group, whatever its size—whether you're leading a Sunday School class, Life Group, cell group, small group, or Bible study—*Small Group Dynamics for Dynamic Group Leaders* lays out a pathway for interactive learning that will help you connect with members for dynamic, memorable, life-changing learning.

The headwinds of cultural secularism, religious pluralism, humanistic materialism, and moral relativism cannot be met by a church that is biblically illiterate, theologically shallow, relationally disconnected, and missionally passive. These headwinds of darkness must be met by people who are Spirit-empowered, Scripturally-versed, theologically-grounded, and relationally-engaged. While too many people are disconnecting from churches, as churches are failing to leave room for intentional discipleship and biblical learning, may the message of this book spark a new commitment to effective group learning that calls us to our highest and best for Christ, together.

Dr. James T. Bradford
Lead Pastor
Central Assembly of God, Springfield, Missouri

*Small Group Dynamics
for Dynamic Group Leaders*

1

JESUS AND HIS DISCIPLES: THE MODEL GROUP

*Our Good Shepherd has become
the model for under-shepherds.
His great concern is the good of the sheep.
A good shepherd gives himself to the sheep.
A thief comes to get something
from the flock—wool or mutton.
Jesus our Lord made every personal claim
subservient to the blessing of his flock;
even to giving His life that they might live.*

WALTER J. CHANTRY

YOU SHARE WITH OTHERS some needs and goals. You interact with these people, working with them in various ways to meet your needs and reach your goals. You recognize a pattern in your relationships, including leadership and individual roles and responsibilities. You feel loyalty and a comfortable sense of attachment to these persons.

This is a definition of *group membership*. You belong.

As you think about this concept, you may be somewhat startled to realize that almost all meaningful activity of your life requires some type of "membership." You are who you are and do what you do in a context of belonging.

> **EVALUATE**   Consider a handful of your most meaningful activities in life. Now identify what groups you are a member of as you are involved in each of those activities. To how many different groups do you belong?

LIFE ACTIVITY	GROUP

> **CONTEMPLATE**   Consider your deepest needs and your highest objectives. What is important to you? What is pleasant and satisfying?

In most cases, you will find yourself thinking in terms of relationships: your family, church group, work group, and friends. Most needs are met and goals are accomplished in the context of interpersonal interactions. This is so natural to human beings that usually it goes unobserved. The highest gratifications come with sharing. Group activity promotes learning and personality development.

> **EVALUATE**   What has group activity helped you learn? How has being part of a group helped to develop your personality? What evidence do you see of your group's promoting learning and personality development in members of your current group?

On the negative side, the most painful disappointments and most distressing problems rise out of interpersonal relationships, faulty communication, and real or perceived rejection—not belonging.

Let Us Make Man

That belonging and togetherness is the natural state of human beings is clearly shown in Scripture. In Genesis 1:26, God said, "Let us make man in our image." The idea of the plural and the idea of mankind are introduced simultaneously. God's creative statements up to that point are translated as impersonal commands: "Let there be light." "Let the land produce...." But the style of expression changes completely with the creation of Adam. It is no longer passive and impersonal but intimate and plural.

The record does not indicate that God was concerned with companionship for the lower animals. But He said it was not good for man to be alone. And, in spite of the fact that God is all-powerful and could offer Adam any sort of assistance, He introduced the remarkable concept that Adam needed a helper!

Our Father...

Jesus said, "'This is how you should pray:'"

> "'Our Father...,
> Give *us* today *our* daily bread.
> Forgive *us our* debts, as *we* also have forgiven *our* debtors.
> And lead *us* not into temptation,
> but deliver *us* from the evil one'"
> (Matthew 9:9–13, emphases mine).

The Lord's Prayer is a group prayer. Perhaps, the prevalent tendency to think of religion as an individualistic experience has blinded Christians to this fact. But the clear implication in the Scriptures is that Jesus thought of His disciples as a group. He thought of individuals as interdependent. His will is that we care for one another.

Who could say sincerely, "Give *us* our daily bread," and not care that another person is starving? Who could say sincerely, "Lead *us* not into temptation," and not care for the young people who are being deceived by modern value systems and social pressures?

3

Thus, in the New Testament, as well as in the Old Testament, the evidence is unmistakable that people are intended to relate to one another, to care for one another, to interact, to cooperate, to help one another, and to share experiences and responsibilities.

What This Means to a Group Leader

From this viewpoint, a study of groups and interpersonal relationships can be seen as exciting and challenging for all Christian workers. It isn't a matter of learning to use group methods and techniques, but rather of understanding how people tend to respond in various situations, and then working with them in cooperation with God's own plan.

This may be called a theoretical approach. Don't let the word *theory* frighten you! What it really means is a set of basic principles that helps explain what you observe and experience. Most leader preparation efforts consist of training and exhortation. That is, Christians are given some ideas concerning methods, or how to do it, and are subjected to inspirational or motivational material to encourage them to put those methods into practice. Of course, these steps are necessary. But even greater proficiency and greater satisfaction in leadership are gained when the leader has background knowledge and is aware of the reasons and principles behind the group experience. In other words, Christian workers need theoretical understanding as well as training and exhortation.

Whatever age group you teach, or whatever your position as a Christian worker and/or leader, a general knowledge of group processes and interpersonal relationships will be useful to you. Feeling that you know and understand will give you confidence in new situations. You will feel more creative and joyful as you develop special ways of dealing with specific persons and problems.

Some Christian workers seem endowed with special talents for group work. And, at times, the sincere presenter of gospel truth may experience special anointing of the Holy Spirit and, without conscious adherence to any plan, be used to effect marvelous results in teaching and leadership. In these cases, the basic principles are in operation and are obvious to an informed observer. (Just as when a person plays beautiful music "by ear" or a person who is anointed speaks in a language he does not know). That such talents and special anointing exist does not alter the fact that most people need specific preparation to work effectively with groups. In fact, those who study and prepare with the motivation to serve the Lord more effectively are likely to find themselves developing natural talents and being used more frequently by the Spirit in ways beyond their rationale.

A major objective of this book is to give you information and a general understanding of theories of group processes and interpersonal relationships. This knowledge will help you feel more comfortable as a group leader and help you to use to the best advantage every opportunity that arises in the group. As you work within the body of Christ, you will recognize problems and be able to help individuals carry out the purposes of the Church. Next to Bible content, no other knowledge is more important to a group leader.

> **CONTEMPLATE**   What are some issues you have been facing in your small group that you might be better equipped to handle by understanding theories of group processes and interpersonal relationships?

In Relation to Social Change

An understanding of group work and interpersonal relations is urgently needed. So many people have been detached from traditional support systems as families disintegrate, work conditions drive people from their homes and communities, and many forces in society undermine people's confidence in values, institutions, and one another.

Probably no other agency is more potentially capable than the Church of providing the group experiences required to meet the real and perceived needs of persons at every age level. It offers opportunities for people to be appreciated, trusted, loved, helped to learn and grow, and to develop the sense of belonging that encourages a positive self-concept as well as commitment to values and objectives.

CONTEMPLATE   What is your group doing to help people...
...feel appreciated, trusted, loved?
...learn and grow?
...develop a sense of belonging that encourages a positive self-concept as well as commitment to values and objectives?

In Relation to Bible Teaching

Group experiences facilitate the learning of biblical content and concepts. That is, people tend to learn better in groups and to retain more of what they hear. Group interaction affects the way personal understandings and applications are developed. One purpose of this book is to help teachers and other leaders use group situations and processes to bring about more and better learning.

In Relation to Christian Growth

Group interaction provides the best opportunity the church has to teach and to demonstrate principles of interpersonal interaction and relationships. These principles are essential to Christian living, at every age level, and to every type of Christian service. Most church problems involve human interactions. Studies in group processes and interpersonal relations will help leaders prepare members and future leaders to relate in Christian ways and work together happily and productively toward Christian goals.

Jesus and His Disciples as an Interacting Group

There is no better description of group formation and development than the account of Christ's ministry as found in the Gospels. Scholars who write commentaries and textbooks are fond of discovering systems and models. But when such a system has been emphasized, it tends to limit other viewpoints. An example of this is the way the ministry of Jesus has been described (on the basis of Matthew 4:23 and other references) as "preaching, teaching, and healing." Almost no attention is given to the distinct quality and style of His interaction with the disciples. This interaction encompasses more than what usually is understood by the term *teaching*. It is a ministry of developing interpersonal relationships and is as essential to the establishment of His church as theological explanations and persuasive preaching.

Take some time to glance through the Gospel of Matthew. It could be described as a report of the interpersonal relationships and interactions of Jesus and His disciples. In eleven chapters, the initial words place the disciples in Jesus' company, directly involved in whatever He is doing. After the calling of the disciples, every major incident and discourse includes some mention of them. This indicates their presence isn't simply an incidental description of the scene. The disciples had a primary group relationship with Jesus. He and they are presented together because this relationship is important to the understanding of the gospel and how it is to be perpetuated by future Christians.

> **INVESTIGATE**   This week, read the Gospel of Matthew. Look particularly for mentions of the disciples as a group. You may wish to highlight these as a reminder for later. What do you notice? What principles can you glean that would apply to your own group's dynamics and relationships?

The Group Was Formed (Matthew 9:10; John 1:29 to 2:1)

The apostle John[1] remembered well the beginning of his association with Jesus. It began the process that would establish the first group of Christian leaders in training, eventually making possible the privilege you have today.

> **CONTEMPLATE**   How did your group form? How did members connect and unite? What was its purpose? How successfully is the group still fulfilling that purpose?

Disciples of John the Baptist, John and Andrew accompanied him to the Jordan River where he was preaching and baptizing. "Look," said John the Baptist, when he saw Jesus approaching, "the Lamb of God, who takes away the sin of the world! This is the one I have been telling you about."

John and Andrew, however, were not content to look. Probably they felt the drawing Presence and a sense of the mission that soon would be the controlling force of their lives. They followed Jesus. Jesus took notice of them. He saw them as persons having some need.

"What do you want?" He asked, inviting them to express their needs or feelings to Him.

"Well...," they must have hesitated. "Rabbi, where are you staying?" In other words, "We know you are a wise teacher. We aren't content just to look at you, and our needs are greater than can be expressed in a moment. We would like to go to your house."

"Come and see," Jesus invited them. He invited them to talk with Him. He allowed them to see where He lived and expressed interest in them. He made friends with them, in the easy, natural way that people get acquainted and then find common needs and interests drawing them together. Jesus laid the foundation, upon which would rest the credibility of His declaration in a bleaker time; He thought of them as friends.

The friendship between Jesus and His disciples is one of the most significant and stimulating topics in the Bible. Friends are not passive recipients. Friends give. Friends share. Friends contribute. Friends accept and appreciate one another. What a model for Christian teachers and students! What a model for Christian leaders and followers!

> **EVALUATE**   What signs of friendship do you see within your group? What can you do to nurture friendship?

Although the space given to the assembly and early development of the group is meager, the pertinent details and implications allow a careful reader to characterize Jesus' methods. Jesus looked at Simon and saw in him Peter ("rock"). That is to say, Jesus saw more than an ordinary fisherman who had a tendency to blunder and act impulsively. He appreciated Simon as a potential stabilizer of the group and its work. Furthermore, He did not hesitate to make His evaluation known. He made a sort of personal investment in Simon when He said, "I see a rock-like character in you." He risked being disappointed or embarrassed later because of bad judgment.

8

Given the entire context, it is reasonable to conclude that Jesus' pronouncement was not merely the prophecy of a divine seer. It was an expression of trust and expectation. Remember, Jesus selected the disciples to carry on the work He had come to earth to initiate—the establishment of the Church (as plainly stated in His prayer in John 17). He was determined to set for them an example that they could be expected to follow, so He related to them in His role as the Son of Man. He *modeled* for them the teaching and leadership behavior that they would be called to emulate in the very near future.

According to the account in the Gospel of John, Jesus called Philip next, and then Philip told Nathanael he had found Christ. Nathanael was a thoughtful and skeptical person. He expressed his doubts about any great person coming from a humble little place such as Nazareth. Nevertheless, he was willing to investigate the matter. When Jesus saw him approaching, He said, "Now there is an honest man." He did not require that Nathanael declare absolute agreement before he could be admitted to the group. Rather Jesus complimented Nathanael for being open in the admission of his doubts! He was patient and courteous, addressing Nathanael's mundane remarks in a serious manner. Again, Jesus was forthright, generous in His words of commendation, and eager to share with His followers the great truths of His kingdom.

> **ARTICULATE**   Consider each member (or potential member) of your group. What potential do you see in each that membership in your group might help them fulfill? Look for ways to communicate your encouraging vision to each member in the coming weeks and to nurture that potential.

Soon after this, Jesus went to a wedding and reception with His disciples. Later He attended a dinner at the home of Matthew, in spite of social conventions that would cause Him to be criticized. Indeed, it might be said Jesus placed himself with His followers, even as He called them to place themselves with Him.

The Composition of the Group

In his comments on Matthew 10, William Barclay calls the 12 who were chosen to be Christ's apostles, "the most extraordinary mixture."[2] He emphasizes that they were common men, having no background or preparation for the work they were called to do. They were individuals who might even have been enemies of one another if they had not been bound together by the purpose for which they were called. Matthew, the tax collector, willing to work for the government that oppressed his own nation, surely could have been hated by Simon, the Zealot, whose passion was to free the nation from foreign rule.

The coming together and interacting of this "extraordinary mixture" of persons is appropriate to its extraordinary position in history. It is the pilot demonstration, the model, the living sample of the Church! The individuals were held together by devotion to Christ and their commitment to His purposes. They had needs and conflicts; they experienced success and failure. They were individuals, and yet a group. That the individuals tended to be common may suggest that status is not a value in His kingdom. That they were "a mixture" (which is to say, a unit with diversified components) may suggest that individual contributions and personal interdependence are blended in Christian community.

> **EVALUATE** In spite of their differences, what do all of your group members share in common (i.e., hopes, goals, needs, strengths, circumstances)?

How Jesus Perceived His Disciples

Searching for Answers and Needing Guidance

From the account in the Gospel of John, it is clear that Jesus thought of those He called as people in search of answers. "What do you want?" He asked them.

They had needs. They were looking for meaning and direction—and probably a cause or purpose to which they could apply their energies.

"Follow Me," Jesus said. These words are best understood as a firm invitation, rather than an absolute command. He allowed them to exercise their will, but made very clear to them the offer of guidance. He asked them to join in His purpose and task. He asked them to trust Him and walk in His footsteps. At the same time, He offered himself to them as a source of direction and assurance.

> **EDUCATE**   As a leader, you don't have to have all the answers to group members' questions and needs. It is helpful, however, for you to know how to direct them to find what they need. Gather a list of resources (with contact information) for various needs you might eventually encounter—local food bank, crisis pregnancy center, community resources, churches and church organizations designed to meet specific needs, Christian counselors, domestic violence shelter.

Capable of Learning and Developing Strengths
"I will make you fishers of men," He declared without qualification. No stronger statement of leader/student interdependence has ever been uttered. Jesus' work required the development of human capabilities beyond the rough skills of survival. But Jesus didn't say, "What you are is worthless. What you are doing is useless." He said, in effect, "I will refine and develop what you are and what you know." He didn't promise to transform them from fishermen into divine oracles. He said, "If you entrust to me what you are and what you know, I will do something very special with you."

Having Potential and Limitations (Matthew 9:35 to 10:8)
As Jesus saw the great crowds "harassed and helpless," He had compassion on them and discussed with His disciples the need for workers. He "gave them authority" and sent them out to minister. It must be noted, however, that He recognized their specific strengths and limitations. They were to go to the lost sheep of Israel, not to the Gentiles. This wasn't prejudice or bias on Jesus' part, but the recognition that these disciples were not prepared to minister in another culture. Ministries especially suited to Gentile evangelism would

SMALL GROUP DYNAMICS FOR DYNAMIC GROUP LEADERS

come later. The disciples were encouraged to use Christ's teachings and the full authority He imparted to them, but within the limits of their own ability and experience.

> **CONTEMPLATE**   Few things can derail fledgling ministry more quickly than failure. Consider a time when you were asked or volunteered for a task that was beyond your capabilities and you failed. How did it affect you and your task? What helped you to overcome that initial failure and succeed? How can you encourage stretching while avoiding placing others in circumstances where they are most likely to fail?

Requiring Patient Explanations and Honest Rebukes

At points, the Gospel of Matthew reads like the account of a teacher with children on a field trip. One can imagine the disciples trailing slightly behind Jesus as He ministered so skillfully among the crowds. And then they run a bit to catch up to Him, a little breathless and filled with wonder. "What did you mean by that, Master?" "Please explain that once more." "We didn't quite hear." "We didn't quite understand."

"Are you still so dull?" Jesus chides, perhaps with a small smile and an indulgent twinkle in His eyes. Then He explains.

At other times, however, the tone of the Master was one of genuine disappointment over the disciples' slowness to learn. He let them know He expected more of them (Matthew 16:5–12).

That we ought to understand Jesus' interaction with His disciples in human terms is most clear when Jesus showed not only that He influenced the disciples, but also that they could influence Him. For example, when He predicted His crucifixion, Peter scolded Him in an impulsive expression of his love for the Master: "No! This will never happen to you!"

Jesus turned and said to Peter, "Out of my sight, Satan! You are a stumbling block to me. You do not have in mind the things of God, but the things of men" (Matthew 16:21–23).

> **EVALUATE**   Patience with group members who don't learn as fast as we might hope and kind but honest rebuke or correction

> may be some of the most difficult—but most important—aspects
> of leading a group. Which is more difficult for you? What are the
> possible consequences of losing patience or failing to confront sin or
> false teaching within the group?

Having Ideas and Opinions That Could Be Respected

The Gospels suggest Jesus discussed matters with His disciples, asked their opinions, and accepted some of their contributions. For example, He seems to have received disciples on the recommendation of others. Andrew "brought Simon" and Philip "found Nathanael."

On the occasion of the feeding of the 5,000, He consulted with the disciples, specifically asking Philip where they might buy bread, even though He already had in mind what He would do (John 6:5–12). Then He accepted Andrew's suggestion to use the barley loaves and fish. He didn't rebuke Philip for lack of faith or tell Andrew that a small lunch was not needed for a large miracle.

Perhaps the most revealing example of Jesus' relationship to His disciples is the conversation "in the region of Caesarea Philippi," when He bared before them all the mystery of His being. He allowed them to answer one of the most intimate questions a person can ask another: What do people think about me? (Matthew 16:13–17). And then, "Who do you say I am?" Now that it was time to prepare His followers for the events of His death and resurrection, the most significant announcement of all time was to be made. And this greatest of all teachers arranged that it should come from the lips of a student. "You are the Christ, the Son of the living God."

> CONTEMPLATE   How free do group members feel to offer ideas,
> insights, and opinions in your group? How can you show respect for
> these and that you value members without allowing the focus to go
> too far afield?

Capable of Being Taught Servanthood By His Example

Jesus knew that His disciples, like all human beings, had some interest in status, personal position, and power. They asked Him on one occasion, "Who is greatest in the kingdom of heaven?" (Matthew 18:1–4), and He showed them a little child. The disciples had heard Him say that the second greatest commandment is "Love your neighbor as yourself." When the mother of James and John had come asking for special positions for her sons, Jesus gave a little sermon on servanthood.

But no illustration, no commandment, and no sermon can cause people to accept this truth of servanthood, which is central to the establishment of the Church and the perpetuation of Christ's work on earth. So, Jesus made himself the living lesson as He washed the feet of the disciples at the last Passover. (See John 13:1–17.)

He said to Peter, "You will understand later what I am doing.... Unless I wash you, you have no part with me."

He was saying to Peter, and to every Christian witness who would follow Him: There is no Body without humility in relationships. There is no Kingdom without servanthood. There is no Church without individuals who work and minister together, having part with one another, as each has part with Christ, and Christ has part with God.

> **MOTIVATE** What are some ways in which you do or can model servanthood to those in your group? How can you encourage and create specific opportunities for group members to serve?

Summary

The objectives of this chapter were to introduce very briefly some concepts of group membership and leadership (which will be treated more fully in other chapters), to lay the foundation for a study of these concepts, and to guide you into an understanding of their importance to you as a Christian leader.

Since God created people as social beings and His plan for the establishment and development of His church requires that His people work together, your success as a Christian leader will depend, to a great extent, on your ability to work with people in groups.

14

A general knowledge of group processes and interpersonal interactions is extremely valuable, if not absolutely essential, for teachers/leaders at all age levels. This means that you need not only a list of methods, but also some theoretical knowledge that you may apply creatively in diverse situations.

The ultimate basis for theory in Christian work is Scripture, and the model offered here is that of Jesus as He led and interacted with His disciples. A summary of such interaction, derived from accounts in the Gospels of Matthew and John, suggests the following principles:

Jesus interacted with His disciples as friends.

He saw them as persons with needs and made himself available.

He saw in them potential that could be developed and openly expressed His appreciation and expectations.

He respected them as individual personalities.

He provided information and teaching.

He guided them patiently, but firmly.

He allowed them to make contributions and suggestions.

He trusted them with important assignments.

He shared with them His values and goals.

He taught them to respect and serve one another.

> **ELABORATE** Choose one or two of the above principles that you most need to work on and develop a specific plan to accomplish them in the coming weeks and months. How will you follow Jesus' example? How will you measure how effectively you are accomplishing your goals?

Evaluate Your Understanding

1. What is, perhaps, the simplest definition of group membership? You _____.
2. What is meant by "the theoretical approach" as it relates to leading a small group?
3. How will a general knowledge of group processes and interpersonal relationships be useful to group leaders?

4. What are some factors that have caused people to detach from traditional support systems?

5. How do group experiences impact learning? Why is group learning important for Christian development?

6. Ministry models based on key aspects of Jesus' example often include preaching, teaching, and healing, but overlook what? Why is this last aspect as important as the first three?

7. What did Jesus see in Peter and Nathanael that showed He was looking beneath the surface?

8. What possible conflicts might have arisen due to the significant differences among Jesus' disciples? What do you think kept the disciples united in spite of their differences? What lesson can you learn for your own group?

9. When Jesus called members of His group, he made a strong statement of leader/student interdependence. What was this statement, and what does it demonstrate about a leader's purpose and methodology?

10. What is the ultimate basis for theory in Christian work and the best model for small group leadership and development?

Activate

▶ Use the principles of Jesus' leadership as shown in Matthew and John listed in the chapter to create a reminder for yourself as you lead your group. Phrase each as a positive imperative, for instance, "I will interact with group members as friends," "I will see them as people with needs and make myself available to them," "I will look for their potential that I can develop and openly express my appreciation and expectations." Post this list somewhere you will see and read it often—on your mirror, bedside table, or as a bookmark in your Bible.

▶ Send a note to at least one group member this week—and a different member each following week—telling them what strengths and potential you see in them and challenging and encouraging them to develop them.

▶ Pray, asking God to help you to better follow Christ's example as a group leader.

▶ Talk with a Christian leader you respect and admire about Christ's example of leadership and how you can apply it to your own life. You may wish to ask this person to commit several weeks or months to mentoring you in the area of leadership.

2

A GROUP IS PEOPLE SHARING

We are not cisterns made for hoarding,
we are channels made for sharing.
BILLY GRAHAM

PEOPLE ARE CLOSE TOGETHER, sometimes touching. They may have eye contact. Most of them have come here for the same reason and are intent upon reaching the same goal. The situation is somewhat structured. Each individual is aware of his or her position and knows what is expected in relation to certain accepted norms and customs. Nevertheless, they may not be a group. They may simply be in the serving line of a popular cafeteria.

On the other hand, they could be a large group, perhaps meeting in the sanctuary of a church. A church group may be much like the serving line of a cafeteria: An assortment of well-prepared and attractive Bible lessons is provided; individual students are nourished; a teacher/leader makes a competent presentation and some students receive valuable information and instruction. (No interpersonal relationships are expected or needed for the activity to accomplish its purpose.)

The cafeteria type of group may provide for each individual at a level comparable to that of a food service line. However, it probably lacks elements similar to what the serving line lacks when compared with a pleasant dinner in the home of loving friends: true sharing. Such interaction is what causes a number of individuals to become a group.

In this chapter, you will get some textbook kind of information about characteristics and types of groups. This is to help you better understand what you see and experience in the group situation. Medical doctors study the whole body in order to treat ears, noses, or skin. Speech therapists must attend premedical groups at college and pass exams in anatomy before they can be certified to diagnose the problems of children who stutter. Christian leaders need opportunities to gain background knowledge that will make them more comfortable and more competent in groups. When you learn to analyze the group as a group situation, you can use Bible content and leadership techniques more effectively.

Group Means Interaction and Influence

A formal definition of the term *group* includes the concepts of interdependence, interaction, and influence. It might be stated that, "a group is a collection of persons who share conditions that make them interdependent to some significant degree, and who interact with one another in such a manner that each individual influences and is influenced by the others, so that individual and collective needs are met."[1]

> **EVALUATE** What conditions do people in your group share? What individual and collective needs might group members be seeking to have met? What does your group do to meet these needs? How successful are you in meeting these needs, and why? What changes might improve your group's ability to meet these needs?

The definition above distinguishes the small group from the random collections typified by the food service line and the large class examples. You will be able to develop a more precise understanding of the group concept if you compare it with some other terms used to designate collections of persons.

- *Groupings.* This term refers to all persons in a category, such as college students or retired persons. In this sense, placing individuals in a group with other persons in the same category isn't what is meant by forming a group.
- *Audience.* This term refers to a temporary collection of persons whose purpose in being together is to observe and, usually, enjoy or learn from what is done by others, but not to participate to any significant degree. What is typically called audience participation is carefully structured and controlled by the leader. Much of what is called discussion and participation in church groups really is audience participation rather than interaction among group members.
- *Congregation.* As used here, the term refers to an audience whose purpose in being together includes corporate activity (such as worship) that is significant to the individual, with or without any true interaction with other persons. Each person is expected to participate, not simply observe, as an audience.

A congregation may become a true group as the individuals influence one another. Group characteristics develop as real sharing occurs, as happens, for example, in an open testimony service. When leaders require response and encourage interaction, for example, handshaking, they are trying to bring the congregation into a group condition and attitude. Although they may not be aware of the principle behind their actions, they realize from experience that most persons respond better and receive more if they participate as group members rather than as separate individuals.

> **EVALUATE**   What types or examples of real sharing occur in your group? What are some ways in which your group encourages real sharing and group development? What can you do personally to

be a positive example of sharing for more reserved members of your group?

Dynamics: The Outcome of Sharing

The term *group dynamics* comes from the writings of Kurt Lewin, who used this expression to describe what happens in groups.[2] Groups are dynamic. They are active, filled with energy and ideas contributed by the members. Further, they are characterized by certain steps of development and processes.

The term wasn't invented to describe what groups ought to be, or how to make people more active in groups. Lewin was a scholar, and his interest was in making observations and then writing down what he saw happening; he recognized a pattern. The study of this pattern is called group dynamics.

Group dynamics isn't a set of rules on how to organize and manipulate people. It is the study of processes by which a conglomeration of individuals become a group. It is the study of how people working together with shared values and goals influence one another and accomplish their objective.

CONTEMPLATE   Reread the definition of group dynamics. How does it relate to what you hope to learn from reading this book?

When this term is used in a course for Christian workers, it means a study of how Christian groups are formed and how people in the church and small groups influence one another. No matter what leadership position you fill, this knowledge will help you to be a better leader and perhaps even a happier person, as you lead some groups and participate as a member of many others.

Characteristics of a Group

Thinking about Jesus and His disciples has given you some practice in using the scholar's method of observation for discovering a pattern.

Similarly, observations and analyses of many human situations have resulted in lists of characteristics of group processes and group functions. Of course, no description or list fits every group exactly, and no evaluative measure says a group must or should follow a specific pattern. However, a group has certain structural characteristics that can be identified.

Interaction

A true group does not exist unless genuine interaction occurs between and among members. This interaction has at least three dimensions. *Physical* interaction includes some informal movement, such as walking about to shake hands with everyone. The leader models interaction by his facial expression, gestures, and other nonverbal language. Seating arrangements that make possible eye contact encourage physical interaction, as do passing around items (e.g., photographs) or serving refreshments. Roleplaying and simulations also provide opportunities for interaction. Physical interaction helps students feel comfortable with one another and be more willing to express their ideas and needs.

Verbal interaction is more than communication between a member and the leader. It is interchange among every person in the group. As has been stated, seating that allows students to address each other comfortably is preferred. Otherwise, it is recommended that the leader move among the members so that in order to see the leader, they must look toward one another. Verbal interaction is encouraged when the members know each other's names and are given opportunities to address questions and comments directly to one another instead of relaying them through the leader.

Emotional interaction refers to a sense of acceptance, of belonging, of mutual interest (see Philippians 2:4). In a true group, members express caring, respect, and a natural, informal courtesy toward one another. They feel free to give honest opinions and are ready to listen to the opinions of others. The development of emotional interaction takes time and must be encouraged by the attitudes and actions of the leader.

> **ELABORATE** Carefully consider your group's physical, verbal, and emotional interaction. Write specific examples of each. Then determine a few specific ideas for improving each type of interaction.

TYPES OF INTERACTION	PHYSICAL	VERBAL	EMOTIONAL
As seen in my group			
Ideas for improvement in my group			

> **COLLABORATE** If you are studying this book with others, ask other members to share what works best for them as well as any difficulties or questions they may have. Much can be learned from the experience and wisdom of the group.

Roles

Since the earliest writings on the subject of human behavior, it has been noted that people not only act as individual persons in relationship to one another, but they also assume meaningful positions, for example, leader, hard worker, information source, healer. This led someone to borrow the word *role* from the vocabulary of drama and redefine it as acting a part that is necessary or functional in society. The word *role* is used in two ways. One meaning is "the behavior that certain persons generally exhibit in the group." The other is "the expectations of the group in relation to certain individuals."

All groups have more or less stable role structures. Although these structures may include formal organization, with members holding relatively fixed positions for designated periods of time, they will include also a pattern of informal roles. Probably you have noticed that certain types of persons seem to appear in almost every group, for example, a "storyteller," a "clown," a "complainer."

The informal roles develop as a collection of individuals becomes a group. Even though the individuals may think of themselves as being similar and equal, role differentiation will occur, for people tend to accept or assume different roles according to their interests, experiences, skills, and personality traits.

The existence of a pattern of role types has been established—it isn't the fabrication of a discipline. Just as many plays have a villain's part and a hero's part, so certain roles seem to develop in almost any group. Rarely are the members of a group equal, and they may be far from alike in tastes, opinions, and actions. In most cases, however, leaders need not worry about this or try to maintain equality and perfect agreement; group members tend to accept roles in which they are comfortable. They tend to be happier and more productive when they know what is expected of them and what they can expect from others.

Role differentiation is compatible with the concept of the body of Christ. It is a term Christian leaders should respect, inasmuch as they learn to respect the differences in group members, and to think of them not in evaluative or status terms, but as persons being developed to play with art and grace the roles they fit best.

More details concerning roles and expectations will be given later.

EVALUATE   What formal roles are present in our group and who holds each one? Which member fills each of these informal roles in your group?

Encourager	Host	Unifier
Organizer	Detail person	Prayer warrior
Optimizer	Welcomer	Loyalist
Includer	Planner	Inviter
Problem solver	Comic relief	Hugger
Provider	Bible answers	Motivator

What other roles do people in your group fill? Determine at least one role (or potential role) for each group member. If one or more members of your group fills a role that is less than helpful, consider what the flip side strength of that could be—for instance, someone who tempers the group's enthusiasm for a new idea might be embraced for helping the group anticipate and avoid potential problems; someone who socializes too much might be tasked with helping newcomers integrate into the group.

Norms

Another characteristic of all groups is that they develop a type of culture. Culture is what people produce as they live and work together. It is the outcome of all human activity. People make things and devise methods in order to meet survival needs. They produce art and music to satisfy their desire for expression and pleasure, and they work out systems of order and control to help them relate smoothly together. The term *norms* refers to these systems of order and control. Norms are the accepted standards by which the group members regulate their behavior.

Norms are usually of two kinds: prescriptive, indicating what people *should* do, and proscriptive, indicating what people *shouldn't* do.

Rules, constitutions, and bylaws are norms that have been written and formally adopted. But even though a group has no formal rules, it has norms. Even random collections of people, such as persons in the cafeteria line, have expectations of behavior. Think how emotions can be aroused if someone tries to push in ahead of others.

Norms can determine what is acceptable in matters of dress and vocabulary, where one sits, and how newcomers are received into the group. They can become the arbitrary basis on which individuals are liked or disliked and their contributions welcomed or rejected.

The most powerful aspect of group norms is that they tend to become internalized. That is, at first, norms may be obeyed because being agreeable and following custom is more comfortable. Then, habitual obedience leads to genuine acceptance of the norm as right and, as the word implies, normal.

For this reason, group norms are tremendously important in the leadership process. When a group member ceases to follow a norm because of external pressure, but does so because it seems natural and satisfying, it has become a part of his value system.

Both positive and negative consequences of this should be recognized by a Christian leader. For Bible teaching to effectively change an individual's life, it must be personally accepted and applied. This principle is in operation in every aspect of group interaction and activity. Not only the Bible content and exhortations concerning Christian living are internalized, but so is the culture of the group. Therefore, it is critical that the leader understand the power of the norms. While the leader is concerned with the official topic of a presentation, what are the norms teaching?

In classic studies of group norms much attention has been given to classifying norms and determining which types of norms are more likely to be formed by groups. From such research come at least two concepts relevant to Christian leadership. One is that group members tend to recognize a norm according to the *amount and quality of participation* actually expected of them. Does the leader truly desire an answer or an opinion, or is it better to be quiet? Is only agreement with the leader expected, or is a divergent viewpoint acceptable?

The other pertinent concept is that the group tends to develop a norm in regard to *social responsibility*. How much are the members expected to care about one another and feel responsible to help or share with them, or to work with them toward the attainment of group goals?

> **CONTEMPLATE**   Evaluate the characteristics of your group related to the two types of norms mentioned above as being most relevant to Christian groups.
>
> Amount and quality of participation expected or allowed:
> - Does the leader truly desire an answer or an opinion, or is it better to be quiet?
> - Is only agreement with the leader expected, or is a divergent viewpoint acceptable?
> - If a person prefers to be silent, is that acceptable?
>
> Social responsibility:
> - How much are the members expected to care about one another and feel responsible to help or share with them, or to work with them toward the attainment of group goals?

- What other norms are at work in your group—consciously or subconsciously (e.g., dress code, common characteristics or attitudes expected of group members, social status, marital status, educational or professional achievement)?
- What might make some potential group members feel as if they don't fit in? What could/should you do to remedy that?

Goals

The fourth universal characteristic of groups is that they have goals. Goals may be of many types and may seem to receive stronger or weaker emphasis in various groups, but essentially every group has a reason to exist. A group that forms in relation to a specific goal will disband when the goal is reached, or it will assume another goal. A collection of persons without a goal is not a true group.

> **CONTEMPLATE**   What is your group's purpose—its reason for existing? Write a brief mission statement here that succinctly encapsulates this purpose.

Most group leaders are aware of two types of goals:

1. Maintaining the group and meeting the needs of its members. This is the internal goal and, in the case of Christian groups, includes spiritual goals for the individual.
2. Working with the members to reach other goals. This is the external goal.

> **CONTEMPLATE**   Outline your internal and external goals for the group. What steps should you take to meet these goals?

Group leaders are interested in both types of goals since, in most cases, they are expected not only to lead one group, but also to assume some responsibility for church goals, such as the spiritual health and growth of the local church.

Some of the most interesting work ever done on the subject of group behavior is that of Muzafer and Carolyn Sherif in a complex study known as The Robber's Cave Experiment.[3] Two groups of boys were studied in conditions of competition and cooperation. The most significant finding from this research is especially relevant to Christian leaders. The researchers found that the most effective way to foster cooperation, group cohesion, and general pleasant relationships is to arrange for people to work toward a shared goal, a goal that cannot be attained without cooperation.

The Sherifs had in mind a practical application for their investigations. They wished to combat racism. The main question was, "Is there any method that will ensure cooperation between two groups?" They tried to bring about interaction and appreciation by simply providing opportunities for the groups to be in contact with each other. Contact didn't cause people to be friendly. They tried authoritarianism, ordering people to cooperate. This method failed. They tried instruction, without success. But they found a shared goal to be the answer. Not only was the goal reached, but people who worked together to reach it began to appreciate and like one another.

> **CONTEMPLATE** How have/could shared goals increased/increase the cohesion of your group? What shared goals do your members have that could be used to further unify the group?

The relationship between group cohesion and goals is vital in all Christian work. Gospel goals can't be reached without dedication and effort, and that combination is the cement that holds people together in mutual support and respect for one another. This was evident as Jesus brought together the "extraordinary mixture" of disciples and shared with them His goal of sending laborers into the vast ripened harvest fields.

Often the secret of maintaining a spirited, enthusiastic group is a matter of goal setting. People need to be aware of purposes and goals in everything they do. The question seems so obvious that probably it is seldom considered, but ask yourself sincerely, "What are my goals?" Then ask yourself, "Have I tried to share these goals, making the group members aware of our ultimate purpose? What can they be or do as a result of being in this group?"

> **ACTIVATE**   Take time to communicate and measure members' understanding of the group's goals and opportunities.

People work together better if they see their personal goals are being achieved as they work toward the group's goals. In the "cafeteria" group, each person may be oriented to think in terms of personal goals. That is, the leader seems to be speaking to individuals, hardly acknowledging the group as a social situation. Development of the group as a group, or body, may be given little attention or none at all. The concept that others are important may never occur to a person in such a group. Some personal goals can be reached without involvement in group goals, but the motivation to cooperate may never be developed.

Since the sharing of common goals is one of the strongest unifying forces, experience in group goal setting and goal attainment is of inestimable value to the long-range development of harmony and stability in the church. The contradictory behavior exhibited by Christians who can't get along with their brothers and sisters in the Lord might be modified by experiences of sharing and the satisfaction that comes from group goal attainment.

One of the magnificent strengths of the Church is that it makes the attainment of personal goals dependent, to a great extent, on the attainment of greater goals. Although the experience of salvation is in itself a personal and individual matter, there is no way to "work out one's salvation" and live abundantly within the will of God except in harmony with gospel goals.

Remember, the teacher/leader must recognize two kinds of goals. First is to maintain the group and meet the needs of its members. Second is to guide the group in reaching other goals.

Types of Groups

Primary Groups

As you read the Book of Genesis, you notice that immediately after the Fall, the Bible account continues as a story of relations in a family. Other histories of human development begin in a similar manner. The first group, the family, is the basic model to which all other types of groups are compared or contrasted.

Groups whose characteristics more nearly resemble those of a family are called primary groups. A primary group is relatively small, intimate, face-to-face. In the primary group an individual interacts and is accepted as a total person. All types of needs are exposed, and the individual expects that these will be met to the best of the group's ability. The shared goals are survival, care of the young, and development of each member through the changing stages of the life span.

Primary groups are support systems, where trust and interdependence are the rule. Interactions are personalized, rather than following systematic patterns. The main type of communication is free and unstructured conversation. The major distinctives of a primary group are physical closeness and psychological intimacy. In some writings this is called a *psyche group*, since it provides the foundation for development of the person.

However, no other group can ever substitute for the family. A person who has positive experiences from infancy in a godly home has the most valuable inheritance. A person who is deprived of such experiences can fully recover only by divine intervention.

Outside the physical family, friends and neighbors do form primary group relationships, as do some other groups bound together personally by strong interest ties, such as religion. It is evident that Jesus and His disciples developed this type of relationship. Jesus prayed that they (and those who would follow them) would be one with Him, even as He is one with God.

History has proved that people absolutely require what the family was intended to provide: the primary group relationship. As population increased, society became more complex, and urbanization and mass media swallowed up simple rural life and family traditions. Many scholars predicted the primary group would be destroyed. They believed that society would become impersonal and bureaucratic structures would replace family relationships. People would come to see primary relationships as a carryover from preindustrial times and would enjoy a new freedom from the limitations of the nuclear family and primary group involvement. This has not happened. Social values and norms change, but the basic needs of the human heart remain as they emerged when God said, "Let us make man."

Support and Therapy Groups

The fundamental need of people to join with others for emotional support becomes even more obvious as the family loses its status in modern society. The number and variety of groups formed in attempts to meet specific needs, most of which were once met within the family, have increased greatly. Almost every human condition, problem, or interest is represented among the groups listed in the local telephone directory. (If they are directed by professionals in medical or mental health fields, they are called therapy groups; if they are not professionally directed, they are known as self-help, or support, groups.)

Today, most people believe that participation in groups can help them in matters such as weight loss, management of grief and stress, personality problems, and adjustment to illness and handicaps. Confidence in the success of these groups is based almost entirely on principles of group dynamics.

Little is to be gained by arguments about the validity of the claims. Rather, Christian leaders should take advantage of any opportunities to get reliable information about such groups. Visit some sessions, if possible, and observe the behaviors of the leaders and participants. Are the members of your group turning to some of these groups for help? Why? Could you offer something in your group that would provide for their needs? Could you guide them toward better sources of help?

Task-Performance Groups

There is an old saying that the Ten Commandments are concise because they were not done by a committee. Another suggests that an elephant is a mouse designed by a committee. Some people declare meetings are a waste of time and people work better alone. Is group work efficient, or is it simply a need in a democratic society to give everyone a voice?

Such questions have been studied and the results show that, although in some situations individuals work more efficiently alone, the group is generally effective in task performance. True, the democratic aspect is important. Specifically, persons who are to be affected by the outcome of a task or project receive satisfaction from taking part in the planning stages and working together to implement the plans. And this group effort leads to improved performance.

Most work in government, education, and religious bodies, and much in industry, involves task-oriented groups. The local church has many such groups: the official boards, building committees, committees to plan special events, regular working groups representing the Sunday school, youth work, women's ministries, to name a few.

The distinctive qualities of task-oriented groups are that the emphasis is on the work at hand rather than the persons, and every member is expected to contribute to the task in some constructive way. Some processes related to task groups are fact finding, decision making, and problem solving. These processes are also related to education and teaching methods.

Are you a member of a committee at church, school, or other organization? As you participate in and observe these groups, you can discover ways to apply group methods and encourage the development of group processes in the group you lead. Also, you may learn from bad examples how to avoid human relations problems.

Educational and Developmental Groups

Have you attended a seminar or workshop lately on finding your genealogical roots, how to cook for a diabetic spouse, how to give "parties" for selling products, or how to be an effective parent?

This category of educational and developmental groups competes in number and variety with support and therapy groups. Although the emphasis is on learning information and skills, proponents rely strongly upon principles of group dynamics to produce results. What the participants bring to the event makes it more effective than reading the same content from a book or listening to the same presenter on tape.

Distinctives of this group type are the *emphasis on instructional materials and methods and individual perception of the goal*. Although the group has no overall goal, each participant has a specifically stated goal and the group situation stimulates him to work toward it. Observation of an educational group in action under the direction of a competent leader will convince you that its dynamic quality depends on group processes and the leader's knowledge and skill in temporarily creating a group from a collection of persons.

> **RESTATE**   Test your understanding. Briefly summarize the purpose, style of interaction and communication, and distinctive values of each type of group. Circle components from all group types that remind you of the group you are leading. What type of group does yours most resemble?

GROUP TYPE	PURPOSE	INTERACTION	COMMUNICATION	DISTINCTIVES
Primary				
Support/ Therapy				
Task Performance				
Educational/ Developmental				

The Christian Group Is a Unique Type

This brief description of types of groups may have you confused. You may be asking, "Where does my group fit?" Or, hopefully, you are inspired by the thought that your group can be a group at once unique and comprehensive. It is not exactly like any other type, but has some of the characteristics of each. It can take advantage of ideas that have proved useful in all aspects of group development, offering the members the benefits of each, in addition to making its own unique contributions.

Primary Group

The Christian group is a bonding center where Christians may develop face-to-face relationships and interact to give and receive support as members of the body of Christ. It is a partner and ally with the home, having the same concerns and objectives for its members and working to supply those elements that may be lacking in the home. For those who have no Christian families, it can serve as a unique primary group. (See Psalm 27:10.)

Support and Therapy Group

The small group is a healing group in two ways. It provides instruction and support in divine healing, and it offers love, attention, and acceptance for individuals with illnesses and problems. No other agency inside or outside the church so completely fits the description of the ideal support for persons of any age or condition. In addition to the essential qualities of caring, acceptance, interchange of experiences and information, and competent, sensitive leadership, the small group offers support and instruction in prayer and guides its members into relationship with the Source of wholeness and peace.

Task-Performance Group

For persons of all ages, the small group provides specific tasks in missionary and outreach projects; social service to those with needs of all types; celebration of special days and events in the church; maintenance of property and equipment; fund raising, music, recreational programs; and participation in the development of curriculum and materials. One of the greatest contributions of groups to the total church ministry is that they can use every ability, talent, and human strength. Any person, regardless of age or condition, who sincerely desires to contribute can participate in some way.

Educational and Developmental Group

Last, and most important, every small group should have as its primary goal to guide its members in Bible-centered living and develop the full range of gifts and abilities bestowed on them by the Creator, that they might serve Him according to His will.

Summary

The study of group characteristics, processes, and behaviors is called *group dynamics*. A knowledge of group dynamics helps the leader understand the actions and responses of people in groups. In this chapter we have covered four universals of those dynamics.

1. The essence of group formation is interaction—each member (not just the leader) sharing ideas and goals. That interaction is physical, verbal, and emotional.
2. Role differentiation is another universal of groups. Individuals assume positions in relationship to others in the group and develop a pattern of role types.
3. Norms are a universal of groups. Worked out by the group, norms represent a system of order and control that becomes the standards (norms) by which members regulate their behavior and evaluate the behavior of others.
4. A fourth universal observed of groups is goals. Internal goals are related to meeting the needs of the group; external goals are related to group achievement. In Christian work these two types of goals combine; personal growth and group cohesion result from working toward the goals of the gospel.

Groups are classified according to their functions. Primary groups resemble family relationships: intimate, accepting, providing for basic emotional needs. Support and therapy groups are formed to help and encourage persons with specific personal problems and conditions. Task-performance groups emphasize external goals. Educational and developmental groups form as workshops, for training in methods and skills.

The Christian group can't be placed in any one category, but has some of the marks and functions of each.

Evaluate Your Understanding

1. Which type of group is sometimes called a psyche group?
2. What are three concepts included in a formal definition of the term group? _____, _____, and _____.
3. What is the difference between a group, a grouping, an audience, and a congregation?
4. How can a congregation become a true group?
5. Group dynamics isn't a set of rules on how to organize and manipulate people. Rather, it is what?
6. Four structural characteristics of all groups include interaction, _____, _____, and _____.
7. Three types of genuine interaction that occur in true groups include _____ interaction, _____ interaction, and _____ interaction.
8. What is the difference between internal and external goals? Give an example of each in your group.
9. Explain the findings of the Sherifs' Robber's Cave Experiment. What implications does this have for your small group?
10. What are the four types of groups mentioned in this book? Which type of group best fits a gathering where this book would be studied? Explain.

Activate

▸ What is the most important lesson from this chapter as it applies to your own situation? How will you apply it in the coming weeks?

- ▶ Discuss what you have learned with another group leader.
- ▶ Clarify and encapsulate with members the purposes, goals, and norms of the group.
- ▶ Plan one activity or course of action you can put into practice at your next meeting to increase group cohesiveness.
- ▶ Pray for each group member by name.
- ▶ Ask God to help you see your group as it truly is, the potential of what it could become, and give you the wisdom and skill to help bridge that gap.

3

A GROUP IS FOR BELONGING

Be united with other Christians. A wall with loose bricks
is not good. The bricks must be cemented together.

CORRIE TEN BOOM

DID YOU EVER FIND YOURSELF moving closer to someone because
you felt uncertain or afraid?

With this small physical movement, you expressed one of the
basic truths about human behavior. People join with one another
both to work out problems and to relieve anxieties, to get information and emotional support.

Have you had the experience of walking into a room where everyone else seemed to be at home and you knew no one? Did you have a
sense of isolation, as though you had lost your way?

Not to belong is to be lost—this is the conclusion of some of the
most influential scholars who study human behavior. This conclusion is interesting to Christians because they use the same terms in
explaining the gospel message. Not to belong to God, through Christ,
is to be lost. Not to belong in the body of Christ is to be a lost soul.

Emile Durkheim, one of the founders of modern sociology, wrote:

> The individual finds joy in it [the formation of groups]. When individuals who are found to have common interests associate, it is not only to defend their interests, it is to associate, that is, not to feel lost . . . to have the pleasure of community, to make one out of many, which is to say, finally, to lead the same moral life together.[1]

Grouping may be studied from secular or Christian view points, and findings may disagree in many of the details, but one conclusion is generally accepted: People need one another and they form groups in response to this need. They feel lost if they don't belong. People associate in order to associate; it is human nature. There is something almost sacred in that thought, for Christian group leaders are charged with a responsibility to understand that the basic need to belong is rooted in the need of people, socially and spiritually, not to be lost.

> **CONTEMPLATE**   How many groups do you belong to? Consider making a list from the very broadest (the human race) to the smallest and most intimate. What valuable benefit do you receive from being a member of each group? With all of these groups that you are part of, why is it still important to be a part of the group you lead? Will the reason be the same for every member of your group?

Social Nature and Early Experience

Most people are born into a group, and earliest awareness involves relationships with other people. Therefore, it isn't possible to separate nature from experience in any absolute way, without reference to divine creation. Even so, many students of human behavior are coming to agree more completely with what is made clear in the Scriptures. That is, they are considering the possibility that people are "genetically disposed" to form groups. They recognize that throughout history physical survival has never depended on the intellect or ability of individuals, but rather on the quality of interaction of people in groups.

Presently, however, individuality and personality analysis and development are more strongly emphasized in American society and education than in most other societies. Some feel this may be the greatest mistake of modern psychology, for it is probable that the true nature of man is social, rather than individualistic.

Emphasizing individuality may not be the greatest mistake of psychologists only. It may be the greatest mistake of the church as well. The fact that each person must accept Christ as an individual has been taken out of context and applied to every aspect of life. Sometimes this results in a feeling among Christians that they are *not* their brother's keepers. Each person is responsible for his own sin and salvation. This seems to lead some persons into an attitude of placing blame and judging others instead of feeling responsible to provide the proper environment (loving groups) where Christianity is modeled as well as preached.

Another mistake (usually derived from poorly taught psychology) that has been accepted by many Christians is the idea that one must love self before he can love others. This is not scriptural. One must be loved before he can love others or develop a healthy concept of self-worth. The greatest commandments are to love God and your neighbor as yourself (in the same manner and to the same degree), not after yourself.

Love is a social concept. God is love. He loved first, and He requires His people to love in the same manner. If He had not predisposed His people to social interaction, they could not have been expected to love one another. There is no such thing as self-love before the love of God, and for most individuals there is little hope of self-love unless they receive love in some kind of caring group, ideally the family.

Transference Theories

Studies of why people tend to form groups usually begin with theories related to early childhood experiences. Since from birth the person's biological and psychological needs must be met through contact with other people, it could hardly be imagined that the person wouldn't develop expectations of interaction and interdependence. To be isolated, to be rejected from the presence and attention of others, is to die. No wonder a baby screams and clings to the parent in fear of being separated. To be alone is like being a fish out of water.

Children are said to identify with their parents. That is, they see themselves in relationship to their parents and gradually develop identity as selves. The parents are the models by which the child's self is formed. Of course, a person is born with some specific characteristics, but even they are tested and developed in relation to the response of the parents. Exceptions occur, but for most persons the family group provides the essential satisfaction of belonging and being protected from outside dangers. Even abused children tend to cling to the known group.

> **CONTEMPLATE**   How are you like your parent(s)? In what ways did your parents' response to you shape who you are today?

According to the explanations known as *transference theories*, forming groups or joining groups is a process by which the family situation, or some part of it, is transferred to another group. Group leaders may be seen as authority figures, somewhat as parents. The group provides satisfactions and opportunities that can be compared to those experienced in the family. Usually, they include a sense of belonging, opportunities to receive information, and opportunities for self-expression and development.

Transference theories are useful in describing the work of the Christian group, since the group should resemble a family in several ways. However, the term *transfer* is not appropriate. The Christian group is an extension of family functions, not a substitute for them.

> **EVALUATE**   How is your Christian group an extension of family functions? Describe specific ways and give examples.

Need-Meeting Theories

People tend to go where their needs are met. This sounds obvious. Yet much time and effort are wasted in appeals for attendance, when attention to need meeting would be more effective. Need-meeting theories are based, like transference theories, on the assumption that people have some specific needs that are met through interaction in groups.

> **CONTEMPLATE** As you study the following material, think of how this knowledge can help you meet the needs of members and visitors in your group.

One major contribution to need-meeting theories is that of William C. Schutz.[2] His three-dimensional group classification system is useful in explaining why people form and join groups. It is adapted here in terms of Christian groups. It is important for leaders to realize that having these five needs met is something that members of every small group want.

Need for Inclusion

From His perspective, God said it is not good for man to be alone. From their perspective, people experience an underlying need to belong in some type of relatively stable association with others. They feel a kind of terror of being excluded, a deep longing for acceptance, and a hunger for communication.

Need for Control

What scholars interpret as a need for control is related to the need to give. People not only seek support for themselves, but they also wish to demonstrate their own strengths and have opportunities to affect the lives of others. Although the unhealthy extreme of this need is the desire for power, the normal need for control is a need to contribute, a need to be recognized, a need to assume some responsibility. Most people join groups with the expectation of having some input. Also, almost every group includes people who need opportunities to develop their leadership potential.

> **EVALUATE** Does someone in your group seem to have a need to control things? How might it help to recognize that tendency as a need to give? How could you involve that person more in giving in order to alleviate the power struggle you may be feeling?

Need for Affection

Probably you have heard someone say, "If he doesn't like me, that's his problem!" Such statements are best interpreted as an indication of the pronounced need people have for affection. Although at times people make determined efforts to prove they don't care whether anyone likes them, don't become offended, impatient, or apathetic toward them. Everyone needs affection. And everyone needs to give affection to others. Of course, unhealthy extremes are possible. A person must be able to accept some rejection and expressions of dislike from others. But a significant and valid reason for the formation and joining of groups is the need to give and receive affection.

> **EVALUATE** Do you show affection to members of the group? Think back over your recent interactions with the group or individuals. Were your words positive or negative? Affirming or discouraging? What do your face and body language communicate? Resolve to show affection more openly.

Need for Protection

Like children plunging into their parents' bed to escape the midnight storm, so persons of all ages seek companionship in times of threat and anxiety. Scholars relate this to a need for protection, but even children sense that usually it is not physical protection they seek.

They seek reassurance: "It will be over soon." They seek information: "Storms are natural in April. It's like this every year." They seek the comfort of knowing the experience is shared with others.

Social scientists, whose business it is to test in some concrete way whatever they feel to be true, have shown that most people in anxiety-producing situations prefer to be with others, rather than alone. In one series of experiments, individuals who had agreed to take part in a scientific investigation were told they would be subject to electric shocks.[3] They were randomly assigned to groups. Those in one group were told the shocks would be severe and painful. Members of the other group were told the shocks were mild and harmless. Each person was then given the option of waiting alone or going into a room with others. A significantly larger number from the severe-shock group chose to wait with others. Also, they expressed considerable interest in gaining information from those who, they were told, had received shocks previously.

Although they don't announce this as their purpose, and may not understand it themselves, people form and join groups to escape or to share the storms and shocks of life. People who are confused and looking for answers will seek group affiliation to reduce anxiety and to gain information.

> **INVESTIGATE**   Explore the needs of group members for protection, comfort, information, and knowledge that others are in the same situation. Prayer requests are a great way to discover needs, problems, and issues facing people, as is social media and conversation over snacks or dessert. Whatever your topic of study or discussion, make time to address some of these needs in a timely manner. Remember, you don't have to have answers or be able to identify with all such needs; almost invariably, someone in your group will have the experience necessary if you will open the floor.

Need for Social Comparison

Did you ever try to find out how much others planned to donate before you decided what to contribute to a gift or project? Did you ever ask others what they planned to wear so you could decide how to dress for a certain event? Are T-shirts OK? May you wear jeans?

This is called social comparison. It goes far beyond donations and dressing. In their search for meaning, people need to compare ideas and feelings with others. They need others to help them interpret the happenings in their lives. Support groups function in this manner. How do others face this situation? What is expected of me now? Questions like these are asked by all people as they struggle to make sense of their experiences and bring order to their world.

The Christian group differs from an ordinary support group, for the main source of information and comfort is the Word of God. However, the Word becomes alive and personal when the members are encouraged to express themselves to one another. They need to test their own thoughts and feelings by making comparisons. If you understand this principle of social comparison you will see a new purpose in group discussion and be able to guide the group more effectively. You aren't simply explaining a truth and making your application. You are providing opportunities for the members to help and encourage one another.

> **MOTIVATE** Encourage all group members to express their thoughts and feelings about the topics discussed. If not everyone is doing so, it may be that you—or some other group members—are making quieter members feel it is not safe to do so. Discuss with the group how to respond to the opinions and feelings of others. Allow quiet members to give insight as to what makes them want to contribute, and encourage other members to do what they can to assist them. Remember, because of the need for social comparison, some people will feel uncomfortable offering their ideas first. Don't push people, but encourage growth and participation.

Exchange Theory

Another commonsense conclusion which has become the subject of formal study is that human interaction is a kind of marketplace. Not long ago it was customary for farmers to trade what they produced (grain and eggs) for what they couldn't produce (sugar and vanilla) so they could have cake. Both the farmer and the merchant naturally wanted a good trade. So they negotiated and exchanged, each trying to get as much as possible for the least cost. A modern example of exchange is the case of grandparents who are willing to give up some freedom in order to enjoy their grandchildren and make a contribution to a young household.

The *social exchange theory* is based on this concept. People form or join groups in order to get benefits, but they realize there are costs. They give up some freedom and forego some individual gratifications to enjoy the group, and also to have the pleasure of making significant contributions.

In a Christian group the principle of exchange is related to need meeting and to role differentiation. That is, as each person is given an opportunity to contribute something, the needs of all can be addressed. Some will be strengthened by giving and some by receiving, as information and experience are shared. This process of interchange is what makes the group potentially an ideal example of Christian community. The leader who knows this will see the benefits, and will prayerfully arrange opportunities for meaningful exchange.

> **COORDINATE**   Write down the name of each group member, visitor, and prospect. Based on your observations, write beside each name what you believe each person has to contribute as well as his or her needs. As you look over the list you've made, give thoughtful and prayerful consideration as to how you might coordinate the exchange of needs and provisions according to the social exchange theory.

When it seems difficult to get the group to enter a discussion, you will recognize that costs are involved. To speak out in a group is somewhat painful for many persons. They are afraid they may be rejected or that others will think their ideas strange. But the lively group is one whose members have found the rewards of sharing to be greater than the costs.

Exchange is not exclusively an adult process. It can be facilitated in some way at every age level. Show-and-Tell is an example of the exchange principle at work among young children. Children are marvelously capable of teaching one another.

Groups Influence Attitudes and Beliefs

Can you think of a food you once disliked, but you now like? Have you changed your mind about a certain type of music, style of dress, furniture, or architecture? Have you come to accept people or a point of view you once rejected? These are examples of attitude change. If you have had an attitude change, can you remember something of the process? How did it happen? Who was involved? As you consider how your own attitudes have been formed, probably you will find that contacts with other people have influenced you. This will give you greater appreciation for the ways in which the formation of attitudes and beliefs can be influenced by group interaction.

Attitudes sometimes are called personal likes and dislikes, but attitude change is more than a personal matter. Millions of dollars are spent every day by commercial and political interests to try to influence your attitudes. The fact that attitude change is such big business is an indication of its importance in human affairs. Probably it is impossible for an individual in modern society to avoid being affected in some way by advertising and promotional techniques. Seldom are the messages presented in the form of straight persuasion, or "preaching," but almost always they involve human drama, dialog, testimony, and interaction.

Christian leaders can learn from this, not to try to imitate advertising methods, but to respect the power of people to influence one another. Leaders must realize that any group experience may affect attitude formation and change, in both positive and negative ways, and that to ignore this fact is to weaken their position as leaders.

You may have heard someone say, "I learned to like her." "I learned to like coffee without sugar." Attitude change is a type of learning. Learning involves a change in perception. You learn by seeing something in a new way. The best learning seems to grow out of group processes, because in interaction people have more opportunities to see how things are perceived by others—to gain a variety of perceptions or to recognize that one viewpoint is accepted by a variety of persons.

Defined loosely as "likes and dislikes," attitudes are made up of relatively long-lasting feelings directed at specific objects (or persons, groups, or ideas). They predispose persons to act in certain ways toward these objects. Attitudes are important, especially in Christian teaching, because they tend to become stable and grow more difficult to change as a person develops. For example, positive attitudes toward Christianity formed early in childhood cannot be changed easily. Failure to establish such attitudes leaves a person much more open to non-Christian influences all through life.

A *belief* differs from an *attitude* in that it relates more to *knowing* than to *feeling*. You believe the Bible is God's Word. This belief leads to your *attitude* of respect and reverence for the Bible. Therefore, if you wish to help people develop the desired attitude toward the Bible you must establish a foundation for *knowing*, and this will lead to *feeling*. Doing things such as insisting that they show reverence or making them promise to respect the Bible are ineffective.

Interpersonal interaction can't provide the initial knowing that is the basis for belief. The leader in a small group provides the solid information and guidance into truth. What the group adds is response to the credibility and competence of the leader. As individuals respond they influence one another. They help one another to clarify ideas, think of questions, and enlarge perceptions. This tends to reinforce belief and stimulate the development of attitudes.

> **CONTEMPLATE** What topics are you currently studying or discussing in your group? What attitudes do you desire members to develop regarding these topics? What knowledge or beliefs are vital for you to communicate for them to develop those attitudes?

Groups Influence Interpersonal Relations

In the teaching of Jesus, only love for God comes before love for others. In that He declared the second greatest commandment is to love one's neighbor, it is amazing how little attention is given to interpersonal relations. Many sermons and lessons emphasize kindness in a general sense, and Christians are taught to care for the needy and give to missions. But real appreciation for peers and the joys of

Christian friendship, amity, comradeship, and coworking often are forgotten subjects. This presents a unique and wonderful challenge for group leaders. The group situation provides the ideal opportunity to help people relate to one another as peers. The group can be a model of love and acceptance, where people feel they are valued and learn to value one another.

Since most church problems involve interpersonal relations, the function of the group in helping people to develop social skills is of great importance to the church. The group does for the church what good families do for the entire society. Those who work together, share goals and values, appreciate individual contributions, show tolerance, and experience true membership in a group will be the most likely to serve the entire church in a similar manner. The cohesiveness, warmth, trust, and willingness to be open with one another—which are the outcomes of healthy group experiences—are the qualities that build a stable and growing church. In small groups, people can learn and practice the attitudes and skills necessary for productive and harmonious work on church committees and other administrative and ministry bodies of the church.

Groups Influence Self-Concept

Sometimes we have prayed for the ability "to see ourselves as others see us."[4] Students of human behavior, on the other hand, have declared that people do see themselves according to the treatment they receive from others. How people "see," or think of, themselves is known as *self-concept*. In modern literature, the term is often given an evaluative adjective, such as *high, low, good, poor*. It is commonly accepted that if children are loved and cared for in infancy, they will feel good about themselves and tend toward healthy emotional development. If they are mistreated or severely deprived they will feel rejected and tend to develop in unhealthy ways. It follows that any positive experience with people can contribute to positive self-concept, and any negative experience can contribute to negative self-concept.

Although such thinking contains much truth, it has led to a general conclusion that low self-concept is bad, most people have too little self-esteem, and most of their problems are somehow the result of the low regard they have for themselves. This isn't true. Most people do not tend to feel worthless and despise themselves. Most people are more likely to "think of [themselves] more highly than [they] ought" (Romans 12:3).

The Bible is the basic source of this truth, but modern research agrees. For example, one study revealed that in response to questions about their abilities, 60 percent of the group rated themselves in the top 10 percent, and 25 percent placed themselves in the top 1 percent. This isn't an unusual case. Experience among students in colleges, both secular and Christian, have shown that many who say they have a "low self-concept" actually make high scores on self-concept tests.

The function of the group isn't to "raise self-concept," but to help people to see themselves in realistic ways. People tend to be unrealistic, to see themselves either better or worse than they are. Self-concept should not be low or high. It should be accurate. Problems result from people's inability to understand their own needs and feelings, to recognize their own weaknesses and strengths. The group can help people to test reality, to find out if their perceptions differ from others. Group participation gives people opportunities to accept themselves and relate to others in realistic ways, thus contributing to the whole body.

The Christian group gives its members the added advantage of testing their perceptions in the light of the Scriptures. Also, the Christian group can provide a picture of God's grace, which is essentially acceptance on the basis of Christ's worth—not our own. The need people feel in this combative, competitive world to justify self shouldn't exist in the Christian group. Instead, the Christian group should offer the opportunities of self-discovery and self-development. Each person can feel free to show what he can do, without fear of ridicule or rejection. And each can admit shortcomings without embarrassment. A realistic self-concept results in positive feelings about oneself without the need to be above, or better than, another, so that positive feelings toward others increase as well.

> **DELIBERATE**   With another leader, discuss what can be done to help group members see themselves realistically without judging themselves better or worse than they really are. Brainstorm ways to make the group a safe way to reveal weaknesses and shortcomings without embarrassment. Remember, a realistic self-concept results in positive feelings about oneself and eliminates the need for unhealthy competition or cutting down others.

Help Newcomers to Belong

In later chapters, you will find more practical suggestions for building the group and helping people to receive the benefits of group membership.

What you have learned so far about the nature of groups, the reasons people form or join groups, and the functions of groups will help you guide newcomers into full membership and fellowship with your group.

Always think first from the point of view of the newcomers. Think of some of the reasons people join groups. They may be in a state of uncertainty or transition of some kind. They may be looking for answers to personal problems. They may feel lonely or fearful. They may be very shy or very forward and eager to make themselves known. Your sensitivity to their possible conditions and needs will help you to pray for guidance and present yourself and the group in the most appropriate manner.

Remember that people usually are concerned about the impression they make, what others think about them. Probably they feel awkward and unsure. They may be trying to evaluate the group to decide whether it will be worth the cost to get involved. They will be wondering what is expected of them and looking (unconsciously) for clues to group norms and values, testing the atmosphere, looking for friendliness, acceptance, or rejection.

If your group is large, having a welcoming committee and arranging a system of introductions is recommended. Never have individuals stand and introduce themselves. And never have a formal routine where everyone shakes hands and parrots some words, such as, "God loves you and so do we." Have the group members prepared to express their friendliness in individual and spontaneous ways.

If you work with children, you can teach them scriptural values and Christian behavior as they welcome newcomers. The biblical emphasis on treatment of guests and strangers can be put into practice. Children's attitudes are influenced more by what they do than by what they hear. Therefore, giving them an opportunity to show love and acceptance to others is one of the finest learning experiences you can offer them. Teach them to express hospitality, to be comfortable in meeting people, and to make graceful introductions.

Whenever possible, try to have some kind of interaction with every newcomer. You may include them and give them cues with words such as: "It is our custom...." "Usually we do this...." Let them know you are aware of them and care about making them welcome, not just by a formal statement, but by the natural, gracious way the group accepts them as well. Don't hesitate to take the time required to help people feel comfortable with one another. Build interaction into your plans, as a farmer would plan soil preparation along with seed planting.

Summary

The major objective of this chapter has been to give you a broad understanding of the functions of groups, that is, what groups do and how they affect people, and then help you to understand the significance of this knowledge in relation to Christian groups.

Several theories from the literature of group dynamics have been briefly presented. These theories, or possible explanations for the forming of groups, have been examined in relation to their application to Christian principles. Among the most significant and relevant ideas are that human nature leads naturally to group formation. Groups are formed and people join groups to meet their needs, such as the need to be included, the need to contribute, and the need to give and receive affection. Also, groups function as a means of social comparison, helping people to know what is expected of them, and as a source of comfort in times of pain or anxiety.

Of special importance in Christian work is the fact that groups influence the attitudes and beliefs of the members. Bible teaching provides a foundation for belief, and group interaction affects the way it is received by the participants. Some ways the group influences interpersonal relations and the development of self-concept have been examined in the light of Christian values and long-range goals of Christian leadership.

Knowledge of group functions and influences will help Christian leaders to understand the needs and conditions of newcomers, so they can be received appropriately and guided into full participation in the group.

Evaluate Your Understanding

1. Which statement is true and which is an unscriptural concept from poorly taught psychology? True or False: One must love self before he can love others. True or False: One must be loved before he can love others or develop a healthy concept of self-worth.

2. What is meant by the term *transference theories*?

3. How relevant and appropriate are transference theories in understanding the work of Christian groups?

4. According to William C. Schutz's group classification system, people form and join groups for what five reasons? Need for _____, need for _____, need for _____, need for _____, and need for _____.

5. How is what scholars describe as a need for control related to the need to give? What are the negative and positive manifestations of this need?

6. The individual's need for protection within the group is less often physical and more often what type of protection?

7. What is the social exchange theory? How does it relate to your group?

8. Why does the best learning seem to result from group processes rather than by lecturing or individual thinking?
9. What's the difference between a belief and an attitude? As a leader, how can you help group members develop desired attitudes?
10. According to the text, groups influence individuals in what areas? _____ and _____ , _____ _____ , and _____ - _____ .

Activate

▶ Consider some practical ways you can help your group better meet members' needs for inclusion, control, affection, protection, and social comparison. Make plans to implement one or more of these before your next gathering.

▶ Discuss with group members how the group makes people feel welcome and what can be done to improve this. Encourage everyone to suggest ways of welcoming newcomers.

▶ Learn to express appreciation for and to others. Set the example and watch others follow.

▶ Learn—and encourage others—to learn everyone's name and what is most important to them.

▶ Consider taking photographs of the group and/or group activities and posting them to a class blog or Face Book page.

▶ Encourage every member to contribute as often and as much as he or she feels comfortable. Ask questions that encourage everyone to share.

▶ When each member arrives, look them squarely in the eye, smile, and, if appropriate, make physical contact (e.g., shake their hands, place your hand on their shoulder, pat their hand). Make every person feel that he or she belongs.

4

HOW PEOPLE ACT IN GROUPS

A genuine leader is not a searcher for consensus but a molder of consensus.

MARTIN LUTHER KING, JR.

"I'M AFRAID I HAVE A TROUBLEMAKER IN MY GROUP," Jim complained to his family as they sat at Sunday dinner. "He insisted on interrupting me just when everything was going smoothly. Said he disagreed with my position and wanted to start a discussion."

"I think that's neat!" exclaimed Jim's teenage son. "Our group is so dull. Nobody ever disagrees with anything."

This father and son expressed two viewpoints of how a group should operate. One (which is more generally accepted in church work) is that the group should be a happy unity, with everyone in agreement and the leader in complete control. Discussion is well directed and the leader is able to manage activity smoothly. The leader in such a group typically says, "This is the lesson," and proceeds to make points, asking a few questions, expecting the discussion to promote the general flow of the prepared material. The leader points out applications.

The second viewpoint is that group members should be free to interact, even disagree with one another and the leader. A leader should be able to guide the group processes, but not manipulate completely the direction of the discussion. Those who take this position believe that learning is promoted by open examination of issues and disagreement can have positive effects. The leader in such a group typically says, "What lessons do you see in this material?" and encourages the group to participate in the development of applications.

Which viewpoint will lead to better results? Important questions seldom have precise answers. Scholars point out that for a minor truth, the opposite always is false, but for a major truth, the opposite also may be true (e.g., see Proverbs 26:4, 5). In this chapter, you will examine some of the fascinating opposites involved in group work, especially the positive and negative aspects of conformity and divergence.

> **CONTEMPLATE**   Are you more like Jim or his son? What makes you comfortable with the style you prefer? What are the advantages and disadvantages of your style? What adjustments could you make to increase learning?

The Group as a System

Conformity and divergence are types of behavior that develop in groups. To comprehend their significance, it's necessary to have some understanding of group processes in general. The term *group processes* is used in two ways. It refers to the group as a total active system and to the actions of the individuals in the group.

Most training materials for leaders have emphasized methods of dealing with a group and how to manage a group situation. Here you will begin by considering the group and the persons who make up the group. Don't think first of how to direct a group, but of how groups develop and how people act in groups. Much insight is gained when you see the group as a system, or combination of dynamic (that is, moving and changing) activities and behaviors, each part affecting all other parts.

General systems theories propose that human activities, institutions, and organizations involve input, process, and outcome. As applied to groups, information is the major input; the process consists of interaction factors, planning, and use of the input to direct the goals; and the outcome is the completed task. In the Christian group, the input is the material provided by the leader; the process is what goes on in the group session; and the outcome is what happens to people, in terms of insights, applications, and behavioral changes as a result.

> **EVALUATE** Describe the input, the process, and the outcome the last time your group met. If you weren't totally satisfied with the outcome, what could you have changed to secure a better outcome?

Major Processes

The fact that almost all human activity and achievement are related in some way to groups inevitably has led to many studies by curious scholars who wish to discover each small working part of the system, analyze and classify whatever they find, and present models and labels to aid understanding. Out of such studies have come a number of group classifications of the major processes. One interesting set of labels is proposed by B. W. Tuckman.[1] He refers to the processes of group development as *forming*, *norming*, *storming*, and *performing*. Following is a brief description of what is included in each of the processes. Tuckman's terms are used here in only a relative sense.

Forming: Becoming a Group

A number of things occur as a group is forming. It is a time of orientation toward others and the situation. Interactions are tentative. People decide whether to become involved. In the case of the Christian group, the leader decides whether to treat the gathering as a group or an audience. If a true group spirit is desired, the leader is in a position to stimulate interaction that will lead in that direction.

A first step in making a gathering into a group is to provide an appropriate seating arrangement. Group members need to see one another. If you use visuals, try to arrange a semicircle. If not, a complete circle may be better. Don't constantly stand behind a speaker's stand.

> **EVALUATE**   What is your group's seating arrangement? Think it through — what are the advantages and disadvantages of that particular arrangement? How can you improve your results and the learning environment by adjusting the seating arrangement?

Next is your own attitude toward the people gathered. Think of them as individuals interacting—not as a unit. It is an interesting paradox that when you respect people as individuals they're more likely to become a group! If you really like the people and enjoy being with them, let it show in your manner. Be flexible. Be willing to talk about real issues. Admit there isn't always one good answer to every question. Encourage individuals to address their remarks to one another, not exclusively to you.

> **RATE**   Rate yourself on the following items using a scale of 0 to 5 (0 being never, 5 being always). The higher your score, the better — especially as your group is forming.

I like the people in my group and it shows.	0	1	2	3	4	5
I am flexible rather than rigid.	0	1	2	3	4	5
I am willing to talk about real issues.	0	1	2	3	4	5
I admit I don't have all the answers.	0	1	2	3	4	5
Members address remarks to others.	0	1	2	3	4	5
I maintain a balance between structure and freedom	0	1	2	3	4	5

Norming: Establishing Relationships and Norms

"Norming" comprises the development of group structure. Formal organization may be established by election of officers and appointment of committees. Individuals begin to assume the roles they will fill more or less consistently, and expectations are formed. Both support for the leader and loyalty and cohesiveness among the members increase. Formal or informal agreement on rules of conduct and procedure is achieved. Consensus is sought and a definite feeling of belonging prevails.

At this stage, the leader should encourage a balance between structure and freedom. Friendly informality can turn into disorganization and fragmentation of the group. This is another paradox of human behavior—people enjoy freedom, but anarchy is painful for almost everyone. The words *liberty in law*, from "America the Beautiful," provide a guideline for group leadership.

Storming: Conflicts and Disagreements

Dissatisfactions arise. A tendency toward self-serving in group activity grows. Competition between members may develop and ideas of others may be criticized. Disagreement over procedures may occur. Personal feelings may distract from the main procedures and objectives of the group. Poor communication and misunderstandings may need to be addressed. New members may not be fully accepted, or individuals may perceive (with or without cause) that they are being rejected. Members may not fill their expected roles or may behave in ways that irritate the group or the leader.

Performing: Performance of Tasks

Members focus their attention on the work or content, and away from their personal feelings and interests. Emphasis is on achievement and productivity. There is increased cooperation and willingness to work together toward shared goals. Decision making and problem solving become more exciting, and individuals are eager to contribute ideas and support. In a Christian group, learning and application of the teachings to group and individual situations are of utmost importance, as personal preferences and self-interest are put aside.

> **EVALUATE** Which stage—forming, norming, storming, or performing—best describes your group's current situation? What

are some of the issues your group is dealing with right now? How does understanding group processes shed light on the situation and help you determine the best course of action?

Maintaining the Group

If you have a group, you can't avoid dynamics! A leader who performs as though passive individuals are receiving material exactly as it is perceived by the leader does not know reality. Not only is the group a system, but each person in the group is a system, influenced by many other persons and groups.

At each group session, the members may be in emotional states entirely different from those of a week ago. They have had new experiences and been exposed to changes in their families or workplaces or both. They have been subject to appeals and persuasive messages, propaganda, or advertising. They may have been ill, or deeply hurt, or severely tempted in some way. Also, there may be newcomers, whose presence not only requires special attention from the leader, but also may affect the moods or responses of others.

Therefore, a type of group-forming must be encouraged each time the group meets. This, along with support and encouragement of group leaders, participation in group activities and projects, and stimulating interest in future plans, constitutes the group-maintaining process. No doubt the greatest challenge to group leadership is the task of maintaining the group. There is more about this in other chapters.

How Individuals Act in Groups

CONTEMPLATE   Here is a brief self-test on the subject of social influence.
1. Would you vote by raising your hand if your opinion were different from that of everyone else?
2. Do you ever express agreement with something you really don't believe just to keep from making an issue?

3. When you hear a number of people make a statement you
   believe is contrary to fact, do you begin to doubt your own
   knowledge?
4. Did you ever speak out in a group to defend a person in the
   minority or being judged by the group?

It makes some people uncomfortable to think of such questions. If you answer one way, you may seem to be conforming to group pressure. If you answer another way, you may seem to be too self-assured, even rebellious. Most persons tend to be conforming in these situations.

The important point for you now is that group membership is dynamic in this way. It exposes people to pressure and helps them to clarify their own values. Being a good group leader does not require the ability to achieve absolute agreement and conformity. It requires knowledge and understanding of group processes and the insight and Christian compassion to use this knowledge to help people grow in Christian ways, as individuals and as group members.

Conformity and Cooperation

You may have noticed that when you look at a light against a dark background it appears to move. This is called the *autokinetic effect.* Researchers have used it to test the tendency of persons to conform to the opinions of others.[2] A person was placed in a totally dark room, and a stationary pinpoint of light was shined on the wall. The light appeared to move, and the person was asked to estimate how far the light moved. After the answer was recorded, groups of three were placed in the room together.

Even though their original estimates were quite different from one another, the three in the room adjusted their estimates and came to an agreement on the distance the light appeared to move. The question was asked, "Did these people change their responses just to be agreeable, or had their opinions actually changed?" When each of them was put back into the room alone to check his original estimate, he stayed with the group estimate. Therefore, it was concluded that each had abandoned his own belief in favor of accepting the group belief. The indication was that individuals' perceptions and beliefs may not be completely their own. They result from the influence of other people.

Whereas the experiments show that many persons actually do perceive differently and change their beliefs as a result of group influence, others yield to such influence in other ways. Some still perceive as they did, but begin to doubt their own perceptions, deciding the group probably is right. Others comply in a completely self-conscious way, deciding to go along with the group in order to keep peace or to be accepted.

Numerous reliable studies lead to similar conclusions. People do have the power to influence one another in very significant ways, even when no real attempt at persuasion occurs. The impact of this sort of knowledge should be clear to every Christian leader. Certainly, they need to be aware of the possible reactions of individuals to group influence, especially as they help people to make honest commitments to the Lord. Conscientious leaders will be driven to their knees in humility. They will offer fervent supplication for wisdom in handling God's Holy Word, and for special guidance in discharging the awesome responsibility of influencing God's precious people.

Roles in the Interaction Process

Among the earliest materials published on the studies of group behavior were descriptions of the various roles individuals assume in the interaction process. You will find such descriptions in most textbooks on group dynamics. Usually the roles are divided into three major categories: group-building (or maintenance) roles, task roles, and self-serving roles.

Group-building roles contribute to building relationships, promoting and maintaining cohesiveness in the group. They involve emotions: feelings of friendship, loyalty, and a sense of belonging. Task roles deal with achievement, working toward goals, and keeping the members involved in productive ways. Self-serving roles are based on the member's individual needs and tend to have a negative, or dysfunctional, effect on the group. In most groups, you will find members whose behavior fits one of the descriptions.

> **EVALUATE** It's important to recognize the various roles each person plays within a group. Consider the members of your group. For each role, select one person who seems to best illustrate the nature of that role.

Following is a list of the roles that lead to conforming and cooperative behavior. The brief description of each role will give you a basis for understanding the behavior of individuals in the group. Sometimes well-intentioned comments from group members make a leader uncomfortable, and are rejected by members, because they aren't understood as group-building or task-oriented attempts. As you become aware of these types of behaviors, you can appreciate the intentions of the contributor and encourage free and positive interaction in the group.

Group-Building Roles

Encouraging—Is warm and responsive to others, accepts their ideas, agrees with them.

Harmonizing—Tries to resolve differences and smooth ruffled feelings.

Compromising—Attempts to make a suggestion that will please everyone, incorporating ideas of several members.

Standard-setting—Calls attention to rules or customs of procedure. Mentions ethics and values.

Following—Is a good listener. Goes along in a passive, but pleasant way.

Tension-relieving—Displays warm good humor. Tries to distract from negative situations, diverting attention to something pleasant or interesting to all.

Gatekeeping—Tries to see that everyone has an opportunity to contribute. Asks opinions of those who have not spoken. Suggests a time limit if some members monopolize the discussion.

Task Roles

Initiating—Suggests new ideas or new ways of looking at the topic or problem.

Information-seeking—Asks for facts or more information.

Information-giving—Provides facts or information. Gives an appropriate illustration from experience.

Opinion-ogiving—States an opinion or belief that is appropriate to the discussion.

Clarifying—Asks for the opinions and ideas of others. Asks for a restatement or explanation.

Elaborating—Builds on a previous comment. Tries to enlarge someone else's idea. Tries to help someone express an idea.

Coordinating—Shows the relationship between and among ideas and thoughts. Tries to pull things together.

Orienting—Tries to keep the discussion on the subject. Defines progress.

Testing—Checks to see if the members are ready to make a decision or come to a consensus about a matter they have been discussing.

Summarizing—Gives a review of a previous discussion or reports an action that has been taken.

Negative Aspects of Conformity

For most Christian leaders, it is difficult to think of obedience as anything but a virtue. But to require absolute obedience and conformity to rules and statements of doctrine must be to assume that those who make the rules and statements are absolutely correct and actually speak for God. To think realistically is to recognize danger as well as virtue in obedience and conformity.

Partly as a result of rapid social changes and deterioration of trusted institutions, many people today feel confused and uncertain. Remember, lack of structure is painful. People seek security. Therefore, they turn to authoritarian figures who claim to speak for God and require absolute conformity and obedience from their followers. If one of these followers tries to disagree or question some practice, the leader calls this rebellion. If anyone outside the following tries to question the practices of the leader, he calls it persecution from Satan. The number of movements calling themselves fundamentalist is increasing as part of the reaction against hollow religion and social decay. Unfortunately, the doctrine and practice of many of them are extremely questionable and lead people away from healthy, authentic church affiliation.

One of the great opportunities in Christian leadership today is to provide people with a foundation of Bible truth and, at the same time, a warm, accepting climate in which they can feel free to express doubts and ask questions. In such an atmosphere, a leader need not be reluctant to admit that some badness can be found in the church and some goodness outside the church. Bringing controversial issues into the open produces the *inoculation effect*. That is, people who are allowed to discuss all aspects of an issue aren't likely to be overwhelmed when they come into contact with those who try to discredit their faith or lead them into some extreme. Another paradox of human behavior is that the desirable kind of conformity grows with freedom of expression.

> **CONTEMPLATE**   Are any issues off limits in your group? Should they be? No matter how uncomfortable some issues may make you, does the inoculation effect make broaching such issues worthwhile?

Conflict and Divergent Behavior

Some people are so afraid of conflict that any small disagreement seems like a problem. Actually, some divergent behavior is necessary to maintain a healthy group atmosphere. Of course, the leader must perceive the difference between disagreement and conflict and be able to convey this to the group. For example, suppose a person says, "I don't agree." The leader should not feel the person is being stubborn, or allow the group to assume conflict exists between the person and the leader. Rather, attention should be turned from the person to the issue. Don't think or say, "Bob does not agree." Think and say, "This is another viewpoint to be considered."

There are two positive outcomes when leaders allow the group to express their doubts and disagreements freely.

1. The leader finds out what the students are thinking, so if there is error it can be corrected. (This is very important in working with young children.)
2. People feel free to ask questions and clear up misunderstandings. They feel more accepted in the group and are less fearful of being put down or ridiculed for their ideas. Trust is developed. (Teens, in particular, especially appreciate and trust those who allow them to express disagreements.)

Self-Serving Behaviors

If a group is generally cohesive, then issue-centered disagreements can lead to positive results. Most true conflict isn't issue-centered, but comes from self-serving behaviors among the members. One value to the leader of this study of group processes is that it provides the basis for distinguishing between issues and personality factors.

Most negative outcomes of conflict can be avoided if the leader is a competent, dedicated Christian who enjoys teaching and models for the group a Christ-like attitude toward people. Business management experts say the best way to solve a problem is to keep it from developing. So, in group leadership, the best way to deal with conflict is to do a good and consistent job of group-forming and group-maintaining.

If some persons in the group seem to persist in pulling against the group and causing disruptions and tensions, the leader must first deal with his own attitudes. Be sure you are thinking of the group and the individuals, not your personal irritations or biases. Make the situation a matter of prayer. Then try to understand the possible reasons for the person's behavior. Sometimes a person who refuses to cooperate in a group is simply seeking attention, but often such a person has some distorted or exaggerated concept of the need to be an individual. Studies have noted four types of individualism:

1. Romantic individualism, or the feeling that it is somehow special to stand alone, facing an opposing world.
2. Egocentric individualism, which puts the emphasis on the need to assert self and not be too concerned with others.

3. Ideological individualism, which takes the position that the only real truth is as it is perceived, and "my idea is as good as yours."
4. Alienated individualism, in which a person feels shut out of society and victimized by the establishment.

When you realize that group members are seeking attention, or that they are expressing some type of individualism, you can arrange to talk to them privately. Almost always, prayerful and compassionate concern will bring about some change in the person and motivate him to relate more positively to the group.

Self-Serving Roles in the Interaction Process

Just as certain persons seem to play more or less consistent roles in building the emotional climate of a group and working toward the group's objectives, so some persons take disruptive, or dysfunctional, roles. Although usually not conscious, the object of these self-serving roles is to meet some personal need. The behaviors of these persons irritate leaders and members alike, sometimes arousing hostility and resulting in open conflict or uncomfortable tension. A leader who understands group dynamics can deal with such behaviors in constructive ways, recognizing them as symptoms of deeper problems. The leader can find other ways of meeting valid needs and of helping persons who are too self-centered to focus on constructive goals with the group. The following are some descriptions of self-centered roles:

Aggression—Criticizing or blaming others, showing hostility, trying to attack the motives or deflate the ego of others.
Blocking—Interfering in some way with the activity of the group by going off on a tangent, telling stories that don't add to the discussion topic, arguing too much on one point.
Dominating—Trying to manipulate others, acting in demanding and authoritative ways, giving directions, interrupting others.
Seeking recognition—Calling attention to self by unusual behavior, loud talking, boisterousness.

Special pleading—Trying to promote a cause, get the attention of the group on some pet idea or project, stir up emotions in regard to an issue apart from the discussion.

Summary

This chapter has discussed group processes, first with the viewpoint of the group as a system, and then in the context of interaction among the group members and the leader. Major group processes include becoming a group, establishing relationships and norms, managing conflicts and disagreements, performing tasks, and maintaining the group.

In the interaction process, individual members assume more or less consistent roles. Group-building roles and task-oriented roles reinforce the major group processes of maintaining the group and achieving the group's goals. Self-serving roles result from attempts of individuals to meet their own needs, and they tend to work against the major processes of maintaining and performing,

In the process of maintaining itself and achieving its goals, the group exerts a powerful influence over its members. The tendency is for most members to conform to group norms and cooperate with group activities. While this generally is a positive outcome, especially in Christian groups, excessive conformity can lead a person into error. The opposite of conformity, divergent behavior, also has positive and negative aspects. Some divergent behavior is functional in a group, but extremely divergent behavior is disruptive conflict.

As an outcome of understanding group processes and roles individuals play, the leader is able to maintain the group and help the members meet their needs in Christian ways.

Evaluate Your Understanding

1. In what two ways is the term group processes used?
2. According to general systems theories, what three factors are involved in all human activities and organizations?

3. What are B.W. Tuckman's four "orming" processes of group development?
4. Why are both group-forming and group-maintaining processes necessary at all meetings? What do these processes involve?
5. Being a good group leader does not require the ability to achieve absolute agreement and conformity. What does it require?
6. What does the illustration of test subjects' responses to the autokinetic effect teach us about individuals' perceptions and beliefs?
7. What are the three major categories of roles within groups?
8. How does one cause the inoculation effect in relation to controversial or difficult issues?
9. What are two positive outcomes when leaders allow the group to express doubts and disagreements freely?
10. What are the four types of individualism?

Activate

▶ When you notice someone within your group playing a positive role (group-building or task-accomplishing), provide positive feedback. Reinforcing positive behavior and contribution will bring more positive behavior.

▶ Evaluate your feelings and what you say when someone in the group disagrees with you. Do you take it as a sign of conflict or as a sign of freedom to be encouraged? Rather than saying, "Bob does not agree," say, "This is another viewpoint to be considered."

▶ If someone in your group is being disruptive or filling self-centered roles, pray for that person, ask God for wisdom and guidance, and set up a meeting to discuss what needs he or she has that might be causing this behavior.

5

UNDERSTANDING AND MISUNDERSTANDING

The art of communication is the language of leadership.
JAMES HUMES

*When they came to Geliloth near the Jordan in
the land of Canaan, the Reubenites, the Gadites
and the half-tribe of Manasseh built an imposing
altar there by the Jordan. And when the Israelites
heard that they had built the altar on the border
of Canaan . . . the whole assembly of Israel
gathered at Shiloh to go to war against them.*
JOSHUA 22:10–12

THIS QUOTATION FROM THE BOOK OF JOSHUA records a misunderstanding that almost led to civil war. Brothers and friends, who
only a short while before had been fighting side by side in a fierce
battle for survival, were ready to draw their swords against one
another. And the real cause was simply a breakdown in the process
of communication.

Probably you remember how Moses led Israel in conquest up to the east bank of the Jordan River. It was decided that the conquered territory would be distributed for administration and establishment of a homeland among the 12 tribes. The tribes of Reuben and Gad, and the half-tribe of Manasseh, received their share of land on the east side of the Jordan. Moses died there, and Joshua was appointed by the Lord to carry on the conquest, westward, across the river.

"You have your land here," Joshua said to the tribes of Reuben and Gad and the half-tribe of Manasseh. "But you must cross the river and help your brothers, until they too have taken possession of their shares."

Willingly, almost eagerly it seems from the record, these tribes agreed to fight alongside the others until the land was taken. The fighting men left their wives and children behind and dedicated themselves to conquer territory for their kinsmen.

You can imagine their joy when Joshua announced, "We now have enough land to make an allotment for each tribe. You are free to take whatever battle spoils you have and go home."

If you have traveled far and returned to an old landmark, you can understand the excitement as they neared the Jordan River. It's no wonder that someone thought of building a memorial and that it would take the form of "an imposing altar." Besides the need to celebrate, the idea had occurred to them that, since the river separated their territory from that of the other tribes, a marker of some kind should indicate that they were part of Israel. They intended for the altar to connect them with their brothers and reinforce the unity they felt after they had fought (and some had died) together.

Exactly the opposite happened. Word came to the 10 tribes that an altar had been built at the Jordan. The leaders were furious. They took immediate action, appointing 10 officials to accompany the priest on a mission to declare war on Reuben, Gad, and the half-tribe of Manasseh. Heated accusations were hurled.

"How could you break faith with God like this? You know we decided that sacrifices and burnt offerings are to be offered only at our official worship center at Shiloh! Haven't you learned anything from seeing the fragmented religions of these heathens? The God of Israel is one God, and we are one people. Don't you remember what happened to others among us who rebelled against the Lord? You will bring down the judgment of God on all of us by your sin!"

The people of Reuben, Gad, and the half-tribe of Manasseh were horrified. "No!" they cried. "We have no intention of making sacrifices and burnt offerings here. This is an altar of commemoration. In fact, its main purpose is to draw us together and symbolize for future generations that, even though we have a river between our lands, we serve the Lord together."

The Scriptures say, "When Phinehas the priest and the leaders... heard what Reuben, Gad, and Manasseh had to say, they were pleased.... And they talked no more about going to war against them" (Joshua 22:30, 33).

Space is given to repeat this bit of Bible history because it is an ideal example of the meaning and importance of communication. Specific applications will become evident as you examine some of the major principles and theories in this provocative field.

> **CONTEMPLATE**   Recall a time (or times) when miscommunication caused problems in your group or in your life. What went wrong? What were the consequences? What did you do to try to fix it? How successful were you? What did you learn from the incident?

Definitions and Descriptions

Probably you have a general feeling that you know the meaning of *communication*.

> **STATE**   Write your definition of communication here.

For most people, this turns out to be more difficult than they might suppose. You realize that simply speaking is not communication, since there must be a hearer. Then it occurs to you that, even if a message is heard, no real communication occurs unless the message is understood. Then perhaps you notice you have assumed a message, so it must be included in the definition.

A classic attempt to pull these components together in an all-purpose definition is Wilbur Schramm's statement of the communication process: "A transmits B through channel C to D with effect E."[1] This might be interpreted as meaning that communication occurs when a person (A) sends a message (B) by means of language or other symbols (C) to a receiving person (D), and the message is understood (E). These aren't the only terms that could be used for the letters, but they form a basis for understanding what is meant by communication.

In one sense, anything or any process that transfers meaning from one person to another is communication. It might be said that any behavior on the part of one person that influences another person is communication. Certainly, it is true the message isn't always in words, and it isn't always consciously transmitted by certain persons to specific other persons.

> **CONTEMPLATE**   Consider the last interaction you had with another person. In what ways did he or she communicate beyond his or her words? What do you think he or she intended to communicate? What do you think he or she communicated unintentionally? What do you think you are communicating— intentionally or unintentionally—to the members of your group?

> **RATE**   How would you rate your communication skills? What are your strengths and weaknesses? In what areas do you need to improve?

For these reasons, the subject of communication is very important to leaders. They need to know what they are unconsciously communicating, as well as how to communicate when they consciously desire to do so. They need to understand the special meaning of communication in groups, where every member is involved in the sending and receiving of messages, both deliberate and unintended.

What is called *communications theory* usually assumes that communication is a process, or system, with six components:

1. *The source.* A person or persons develop an intent to communicate. For example, a person has in mind an idea, a request, some information, a command, a Bible lesson, with intent to convey it to a receiver. At this point the source has only a mental conceptualization, emotion, and a desire to transmit.
2. *The message.* The intent is put into message form, that is, language and symbols are selected as a means by which the intended idea or information can be transmitted to the receiver.
3. *The channel.* A method of presentation is selected. This may be a medium or a style of speaking. Sometimes it includes a type of clothing to be worn. For example, if you were applying for a job, you would dress differently than if you were going next door to welcome new neighbors.
4. *The receiver.* This is the person or persons who receive the message. The message comes as a sense perception, through hearing and/or vision, and then it is "decoded," or interpreted, from the physical stimuli and becomes the message as perceived by the receiver.
5. *Feedback.* This is the return process, as the receiver responds to the message. From this, the source is able to know how the message was interpreted. Usually the source can determine from the feedback whether the message was understood. Feedback is important in teaching, since it gives the leader opportunities to repeat ideas or to change methods if the message isn't being understood. (This is one reason why a straight lecture or media message usually is less effective than a method that allows for feedback.)
6. *Barriers.* Between the meaning intended by the source and the meaning perceived by the receiver many barriers may exist. Obstacles to understanding and interpretation may cause the message to be distorted or modified in some way. Information or language may be unclear, or the persons who are trying to

communicate may have widely divergent viewpoints, experiences, or personality traits.

> **EVALUATE**   What are some barriers to good communication within your group? How can you remove or overcome these barriers and improve communication?

The Importance of Communication

The first step toward good communication is to recognize its importance. Sometimes marriage problems arise, not because couples are unable to communicate, but because they haven't really tried. Each party acts in a unilateral way, expecting the other to understand, or not realizing that some explanation should be offered. Leaders make the same kind of mistake. They ignore people's need to be informed and don't understand that they may be transmitting unintended messages or not making an effort to communicate at all.

The communication problem among the tribes of Israel began with the failure of Reuben, Gad, and the half-tribe of Manasseh to share their plans with the others. If they had thought to send a messenger to Shiloh to explain the purpose of the altar and ask their kinsmen to participate in the victory ceremonies, then no misunderstanding would have arisen.

A mark of great leadership is willingness to share plans and ideas. Warm empathy and respect for people are indicated when leaders explain their actions. This is an aspect of the role of friend—which Jesus assumed among His disciples. He did not plunge ahead, taking them for granted, expecting them to follow blindly. He took time to explain things beforehand, not only to give directions and assignments, but to include them in the planning.

Helping people feel included is a special function of communication in group building and group maintaining. Don't walk in, smugly prepared and self-sufficient, at exactly the right moment, and begin a session in an impersonal manner. Look for opportunities to communicate. Talk about your plans and hopes for the group. Tell the members when you are pleased and when you are concerned. Ask their opinions. Ask them to pray and to make suggestions.

> **DEMONSTRATE** It takes a strong leader to be willing to share plans and ideas with the group and allow them input, as we are never certain how it will go or where we will end up. Still, the return on this type of communication—making members feel valued and included—is well worth the effort and uncertainty. What are your most recent thoughts and plans for your group's future? Demonstrate your love and friendship with the group by making a plan to communicate with them and solicit their input before you finalize the plan. You'll find that when people buy into your plan and feel a part of it, there will be greater unity and leading will be much simpler.

Effective Communication

No doubt you have heard it said of one speaker or another, he is "an excellent communicator of the gospel." Probably someone means by this that the person speaks well and attracts large audiences. It might be surprising, however, to learn how much deliberate communication actually happens.

To investigate this question, a group of researchers visited the homes of people who had attended church on a day the minister spoke on the subject of racial prejudice. When asked whether they had heard or read anything about racial prejudice in the recent past, only 10 percent spontaneously recalled the sermon. When the remaining 90 percent were directly asked whether their minister had said anything about racial prejudice, over 30 percent answered no. The experiment was repeated in 12 churches, to eliminate the possibility that results were based mostly on the style or ability of one minister.

The point of this is that the task of communicating is not simple. Those concerned with how to communicate more effectively tend to focus on the source person and the techniques of speaking and platform personality. But as a group leader, you need not be a great

SMALL GROUP DYNAMICS FOR DYNAMIC GROUP LEADERS

performer. Results of the research indicate that much of your attention should be given to principles related to the message, the receiver, and barriers that block communication.

Making the Message Clear

Have you worked a jigsaw puzzle? Did you ever try to work one when the box had been lost and you had no idea what picture you were trying to build? Probably you prefer to see the picture before you start work on the puzzle. Similarly, it is easier to make a message (or lesson) clear to the listeners if you have the expected end in your mind before you begin. You "picture," or conceptualize, the desired outcomes or purposes of a message. In lesson preparation, this means writing specific objectives. No doubt you are well aware of the value of an outline. Objectives are even more important than outlines and must be determined before an outline is begun. Many attempts at communication fail because the source person tries to outline a message without having objectives clearly in mind.

To write clear objectives, you must be confident in your knowledge of the subject, and you must know the receivers well enough to put together objectives appropriate to their ability. When you have decided on suitable objectives, then outline the material so it leads toward them.

Finally, you must select words and illustrations that will cause the receivers to see the same picture you have in mind. It was failure "to see the same picture" that caused the 10 tribes to become incensed at their brothers' building an altar by the Jordan. The pictures were totally different. The altar meant "sacrifice and burnt offerings" to the 10 tribes, and "a symbol of fraternity" to Reuben, Gad, and the half-tribe of Manasseh. When the 10 tribes listened to the other tribes' interpretation of the symbol, communication was achieved and understanding was restored. And they "gave the altar this name: A Witness Between Us That the Lord Is God" (Joshua 22:34).

> **CREATE** Use the guidance from this section to plan your next study. Start with clear objectives of what you hope to accomplish

based on your knowledge of the subject and the group's abilities and interests. Next, outline your material so it leads to fulfilling your objectives. Finally, select words and illustrations to help group members to see the same picture you have in mind.

Some Types of Receivers

When you think of effective communication from the point of view of the source person, you are likely to fall into the formula trap. That is, you will try to devise a formula, or model, for the effective message. It may go something like this: Begin with a good story to get attention. Use many illustrations. Keep on the main point, and avoid small facts and details. Be inspirational. The formula assumes that all receivers can be reached in the same way.

Actually, receivers are of distinct types. A good communicator tries to think from the point of view of receivers, for at least three reasons. First, a presentation may be planned to appeal to several types. Second, knowledge of different receiver types will help the leader understand why group members seem to respond in different ways. Third, the leader can help the different types to interact, appreciate one another, and learn from one another.

This is one of the exciting challenges of group work. Four types of receivers have been described. They are what are called ideal types. That is, few individuals fit completely and at all times into one type. Even so, the group classification is helpful as you try to meet the needs of each person and maintain good interpersonal relations.

1. *Thinking people.* Interested in facts and logic, they may become impatient with a leader who tells many stories. They don't want more examples. They want reasons, explanations, and opportunities to ask detailed questions. They prefer to make their own applications.
2. *Feeling people.* Needing emotional inspiration and challenge, they appreciate illustrations that are intimate and personal. They may become bored with facts and logical or theoretical

explanations. They may expect moral and spiritual applications to be supplied by the leader.

3. *Sensing people.* Especially fond of media presentations, they also enjoy games, demonstrations, and simulations. They may become restless or inattentive when there seems to be too little action.
4. *Intuitive people.* Quick to jump to conclusions, they also look for hidden meanings and point out alternative applications and points of view. They need opportunities to express original ideas and are impatient when things seem too cut and dried.

> **EVALUATE** Consider the members of your group. What types of receiver do you think they may be? If you are unsure about any, make it a goal to interact with him or her to better understand their learning type.

Barriers to Communication

As you can see, an intended communication has a precarious journey from source to receiver. Putting together a message and selecting a method of presentation must be done with care. The receiver must be alert, resist jumping to conclusions, comprehend the message—then choose to accept or reject it. And in the case of a message such as a lesson, the communication is effective only when the receiver remembers it and puts it into practice in some significant manner. Barriers to communication may block or modify the message at any of these points—attending, comprehending, believing (or accepting), remembering, and putting into practice. Some barriers to communication are the following:

- *The consciousness of the receiver.* The receiver may not pay attention because of an emotional or physical state, or because the message or style of delivery awakens no interest.
- *Language.* Many words and expressions have more than one meaning. Remember the difficulty Nicodemus had with the term *born again*? (John 3:1-12). Terms change in meaning with

changing social values and conditions. Leaders need to keep up with the language of children and teens. A common example is that to many modern children the use of the title *Father* evokes fear and dislike rather than love and protection.

- *Symbols.* Symbols are so much a part of the communication of the gospel that leaders may fail to realize they aren't understood by many newcomers. Essential symbolism (such as the Lord's Supper) must be explained to children as simply as possible, and most other symbolism should be avoided for children under the age of 6 or 7.
- *Mixed messages.* Communication is impeded when body language seems to contradict words. For example, a child came to mistrust a teacher who said she loved the Bible and then threw it carelessly into a corner.

EVALUATE Consider videoing yourself as you speak or lead your group, and then watch and critique it closely. Are you sending any mixed messages? What are your body language, facial expressions, tone of voice, and interaction with others communicating that you might not have realized?

- *Customs.* Sometimes persons have trouble understanding the verbal and nonverbal messages of others whose customs are different. This can be avoided if newcomers are made aware of local customs and are warmly invited to share experiences and information with the group.
- *Prejudice.* People can't communicate effectively with persons they don't accept as equals. One scriptural example is that of the Israelites and the Samaritans. Because the Israelites generally considered Samaritans and all Gentiles inferior to themselves, the gospel could not be communicated freely. For this reason, the Lord spoke to Peter in a vision and guided him in overcoming the barrier of prejudice (Acts 10).
- *Status, age, and sex.* Most people find it more difficult to communicate with those in positions that society considers

lower or higher than their own. For example, some wealthy Christians find witnessing to their employees impossible, and some Christian employees find witnessing to their employers equally impossible. Older and younger persons may find communication with one another difficult. And communication between males and females may tend to be strained.

Group leaders must learn to be comfortable communicating with all members and help to eliminate the barriers to group interaction.

CONTEMPLATE   What barriers may be hindering good communication in your group?

Receiver Response to the Message

As you consider the processes of response to messages, you become aware that effective communication is more than speaking ability. One of these processes is *perception*, which refers to the individual and personal interpretation of the message. Another is *attribution*, which refers to a motive or condition inferred by the receiver.

Perception

You remember that it was not what the eastern tribes did that put Israel on the brink of civil war. Rather, it was how the western tribes *perceived* the action. How many misunderstandings would never become disputes if people would ask themselves, "Do I perceive the message as it is intended?"

Leaders who are unaware of the process of perception may be shocked by responses from their students. A typical example is that of the teacher who was trying to explain to her preschool children the plight of the hungry prodigal in the pigpen. A bright youngster interrupted with a logical question: "Why didn't he butcher a pig?"

The child perceived the situation from what is known as her *field of experience*: Her father was a butcher by trade, and she had visited her grandfather's farm at butchering time. The teacher, whose field of experience contained nothing of meat that was not prewrapped in plastic at the supermarket, had never considered the possibility that was evident to the child.

The lesson carried away from the group session seldom is exactly the same as the one intended by the leader. Rather it is the one perceived by the student. All perception is dependent on one's field of experience, and communication is dependent on a field of experience shared by the source and the receiver. Language is the basic shared experience. Whatever a leader can do to enlarge the shared area of experience makes communication more effective.

Attribution

Related to perception is the *process of attribution*. The interpretation of any message is affected by motives attributed to the source. A message intended to be persuasive is much less powerful when the receiver believes he is being manipulated. An indirect approach, where the speaker doesn't seem to have a personal interest in the matter, is more effective. The final consequence of a message frequently depends on the process of attribution, more than on the content of the message itself. For example, the amount of an offering may depend, not upon the actual need or worthiness of the cause, but upon the motives attributed to the one who takes the offering.

Attribution is the underlying process in many disputes and misunderstandings. Just as the western tribes jumped to a hasty conclusion and accused their kinsmen of breaking faith and rebelling against God, so are people quick to attribute motives when they feel confused or threatened by the behavior of others. Good communication requires that situations be observed and described objectively, without reading in motives.

Listening Is a Part of Communication

"When Phinehas the priest and the leaders... *heard* what Reuben, Gad, and Manasseh had to say, they were pleased... and they talked no more about going to war against them" (Joshua 22:30–32, emphasis mine).

Group work has an advantage over any other structured method of gospel presentation, if the leader will use it effectively. That advantage is the opportunity to listen. Active listening by the leader is a signal of respect and appreciation of the members. It helps to stimulate participation and lively interaction. It encourages members to disclose their problems and seek guidance. And it is the only way a leader can gain some control over the processes of perception and attribution.

Group interaction brings to light perceptions that would never be discovered in another setting, perceptions that could change the direction of a person's life. Incorrect perceptions can be modified, and perceptions that are imaginative and enlightening can be shared with others. Open discussion and the modeling of the leader promote understanding and acceptance, so that people are less prone to make inappropriate attributions and misunderstand one another.

As leaders listen and teach others how to listen to one another, the shared field of experience is enlarged. People become more sensitive to the feelings of others, more accepting of diverse personality traits, more open to the opinions and viewpoints of others. Mutual needs and goals are recognized. Petty anxieties that divide people are forgotten when they really hear one another, and the foundation for true Christian community is established.

Summary

A distinct advantage of the group in Christian teaching and learning is that it can encourage the development of interpersonal communication. On the other hand, group leadership requires an understanding of the processes and principles of communication. Major objectives of this chapter have been to present some essential facts and theories in the field of communication, and to help the leader use them to communicate more effectively and promote communication in the group.

It has been stressed that communication is not merely platform technique; understanding interpersonal and group processes is as necessary to good communication as are presentation skills.

The communications process includes the source, the message, the channel, the receiver, feedback, and barriers to communication. Effective communication depends on the ability of the source person to conceptualize the message accurately, frame the message appropriately, understand something of the character and condition of the receiver, and overcome the barriers. The objective of communication is to have the message reach the receiver as it is intended by the source person.

Good communication not only facilitates the transmission of messages, but also promotes understanding and appreciation in the group. Leaders have opportunities not available in other situations to find out how messages are perceived. Therefore, they can help students to interpret the lesson material and also the intended, and unintended, messages group members send to one another.

Evaluate Your Understanding

1. Go back to your definition of communication from the beginning of the chapter. How has your understanding changed? Write down a new definition.
2. According to communications theory, what are the six components of communication?
3. The communication problem among the tribes of Israel with the building of the altar began with what failure?
4. Which of the six components of communication do leaders tend to focus on, and, according to research, what aspects would we be wiser to focus on?
5. In lesson preparation, what is the importance of an outline and objectives? Which must come first?
6. What are the four types of receivers and how does each learn best?
7. What are three reasons a good communicator tries to think from the point of view of various types of receivers?
8. Barriers to communication may block or modify the message at any of what points?

9. What are perception and attribution, and how do they affect what message hearers receive?
10. What are some of the advantages of listening to your group?

Activate

▶ If you are aware of any miscommunications within your group, take deliberate steps to correct the problems and communicate clearly.

▶ Don't get stuck in a rut! While planning your group meeting, consider the different learning styles. Be sure you choose methodologies, formats, words, and illustrations to communicate that will appeal variously to all of the styles.

▶ Consider asking a trusted colleague or friend to attend your group and give you feedback on your communication. What are you doing well? How might you improve?

▶ Ask God to help you better communicate His love and His message to members of your group.

6

THE LEADERSHIP ROLE IN TEACHING

A leader is one who knows the way,
goes the way, and shows the way.
JOHN C. MAXWELL

Moses said to the Israelites, "See, the Lord has
chosen Bezalel... and he has filled him with the
Spirit of God, with skill, ability, and knowledge in
all kinds of crafts—to make artistic designs.... And
he has given... him... the ability to teach others"
EXODUS 35:30-34

MOSES, GOD'S CHOSEN LEADER, acted as a kind of talent scout to select others to whom God had given various abilities. He organized these gifted ones into teams of teachers and craftsmen. Together they produced all the articles for the tabernacle and the priestly garments for Aaron, the high priest.

Do you not believe that the Lord who created the wondrous beauty of the universe could have sent down from heaven a glorious priestly garment for Aaron? But such action would never fit God's plan. With the creation of human beings, God stated that His plan is people. He outlined precisely the first "theory" of leadership when He made Adam His partner to name the animals and care for the earth. From then until now, God has elected to work through people, usually choosing a leader—like Moses—to enlist, organize, and support other people in the accomplishment of some task or the attainment of some goal.

The ultimate indication that God's plan involves a leadership theory is the fact that His revelation to people is entrusted to teachers. In the preparation of the tabernacle, God did not have individuals simply start to work and expect the Holy Spirit to direct them into artistic productions. He elected to have the most skilled ones teach others. Why do so many Christians miss the marvel of this? It's a wonder that teachers don't fall on their faces in humility and appreciation, awestruck that God would use them to carry out His plan!

Those who study human behavior may not acknowledge God, but they recognize that teaching and leading are built into the nature of mankind. Scholars study what they see, and they have been intrigued with the prevalence of a leadership pattern in every type of human activity. They began with studies of defined groups, such as committees, boards, and juries, where a leadership role is built into the structure. But soon it became apparent that a leadership role develops in the most informal gatherings. Whenever people feel a need for coordination, administration, or problem-solving of any type, one person in the group will emerge as the leader. Notice this interesting process next time you eat out or go on a trip with a group or get together in any impromptu situation. The indications are that leadership is one of the few universals of human behavior, present in all known societies.

The purpose of this chapter isn't to teach you specific techniques for leading people. Some practical applications are suggested, and more will be given in the last four chapters. But now you will think about the nature and function of leadership and your place as a Christian leader.

Leadership Isn't Easy to Define

Although it is observed constantly, the nature of leadership is difficult to describe, and the concept is widely misunderstood.

| **STATE**   What is leadership? Write down your definition.

People speak of leadership as though it were a process of control over others, or a high position demanding special privileges. Actually, dictators, bosses, and star performers aren't really leaders.

The term *leader* includes the idea of interaction and relationship with others in the pursuit of some objective all wish to achieve. The leader provides a climate in which group members develop enthusiasm, are motivated to exert energy, and find individual as well as group satisfactions. Thus, the term *leadership* refers more to a process of influence than to a person. A Christian leader is a person who stimulates and develops the capacities of others and guides them in the attainment of Christian goals.

Attracted by the fascinating and elusive nature of the subject, hundreds of curious researchers have analyzed group situations in efforts to describe what leaders are like, what their functions are, what behaviors are most effective, how groups react to various types of leadership, and other related questions. On the basis of such inquiries, numerous theories of leadership have been proposed. Many of the studies relate to business management, committee work, and group counseling. However, most of the findings apply to the nature and process of leadership wherever it is found. Certainly, this includes the group room, where the leader is constantly challenged to fill a dual role.

The Teacher as a Leader

Teaching and leading are somewhat like the motor and the fuel in an automobile. You can describe the two separately, but you can't go anywhere without both. Leaders find it necessary to do some teaching in order to accomplish their purposes, and teachers must exercise leadership skills to accomplish theirs.

In general, the difference between leadership and teaching is one of proportion. The leader places more emphasis on the process; the teacher places more emphasis on content. In actual practice, even this distinction may be obliterated in the case of the teacher. In that complex interaction called teaching and learning, where mental, emotional, and social forces combine in ever-changing patterns, what happens to the content may depend entirely on the process. That's why teachers study theories and principles of group leadership.

Most of the earliest studies tried to define leadership in terms of traits or characteristics of leaders. Thousands of pages have been written on this subject, but the only conclusion upon which there is any agreement is that some successful leaders have one set of characteristics and some have another. There is no typical leader. However, if you go through the lists of traits from several sources, you will find some repeated more often than others. These most-agreed-upon traits of good leaders are remarkably consistent with biblical principles of human relations and leadership. By adding three specifically Christian traits,* the list forms a set of ideal characteristics, or a model, by which Christian leadership might be described.

Characteristics of Christian Leaders

As you briefly consider each of the ideal traits below, notice that they are consistent with the leadership behavior of Jesus as presented in chapter 1.

> **INVESTIGATE**   As you consider each of the ideal traits of leadership that follow, fill in the following chart.

IDEAL TRAIT	HOW JESUS DEMONSTRATED IT	HOW I MEASURE UP
Empathy		
Goal achievement		

IDEAL TRAIT	HOW JESUS DEMONSTRATED IT	HOW I MEASURE UP
Competence		
Emotional stability		
Group membership		
Ability to share leadership		
Consistency and dependability		
*A sense of God's calling		
*Dependence on the Holy Spirit's guidance		
*Exemplary living in accordance with Christian moral and ethical standards		

Empathy Good leaders can see things from another person's point of view. They try to understand how others feel. Teachers have a unique challenge, in that they must try to view things from the perspective of children, teens, singles, elderly, bereaved persons, and many other individuals and groups. "Do to others as you would have them do to you" (Luke 6:31). "Remember those in prison as if you were their fellow prisoners, and those who are mistreated as if you yourselves were suffering" (Hebrews 13:3).

Goal achievement Good leaders are able to set goals and work toward them until they are achieved. They enjoy having goals. They set goals for themselves and their groups. Good leaders are purposeful: "I press on toward the goal to win the prize for which God has called me heavenward in Christ Jesus" (Philippians 3:14).

Competence Good leaders do their work well and take advantage of every opportunity to gain knowledge and improve their skills. They work hard and set high standards for themselves and for those they lead. They expect the best from others and respect the competence of others. The Scriptures contain many references to the need for skill and diligence in the Lord's work. Some examples are Exodus 35 and 36; Proverbs 12:27; 22:29; 31:10–31; and 2 Timothy 2:15.

Emotional stability Good leaders are reasonable, confident, and cheerful. They don't get angry easily, are not willful, moody, or easily discouraged. They can act in a peaceful, gracious manner in unexpected situations, when plans fail or people disappoint them. They don't display petty hurts, blame others, or embarrass others in a group. The Psalmist David expresses this concept when he declares that in all trouble he is still confident and will sing praises. "Be strong and take heart" (Psalm 27:14).

> **CONTEMPLATE** Have you ever had a teacher or group leader whose emotional instability negatively impacted the group? What was it like for those trying to learn? What did that experience teach you about leadership?

Group membership Good leaders have a strong sense of being a part of the group. They are aware of a common interest and like working with others. They deeply appreciate the relationship. Absolutely essential to Christian leadership is the understanding that individuals, like parts of the body, find their true life and usefulness when they are "joined and held together by every supporting ligament" (Ephesians 4:16). Leaders exist only in relationship to the group. For leaders of teens, the development of this body relationship and sincere feeling of common interest are extremely important, since adolescents tend to become alienated from their leaders.

Ability to share leadership Good leaders work well with their groups—and also with other leaders. Most Christian leaders are *middle leaders*. Much discomfort and misunderstanding in Christian work results from failure to understand this unique position. Middle leaders follow others with loyalty and respect, and know how they fit into the general organizational plan. Also, they have high regard for the group members and give them opportunities to exercise their leadership abilities whenever it is appropriate. The gifts and callings of all are appreciated and acknowledged. "Submit to one another out of reverence for Christ" (Ephesians 5:21). Paul sets the example for leaders in his frequent expressions of appreciation for his coworkers and helpers. Examples are recorded in Philippians 4:13, Colossians 4:7–14, 1 Thessalonians 1:2–4.

Consistency and dependability Good leaders communicate in a clear, honest way, and act in accordance with their words. The group knows what to expect from the leader, and what the leader expects from the members. Good leaders don't get enthusiastic about a project and then change their minds and do something different without informing the group. They keep their word and abide by the same norms and standards expected of others. They can be relied on. They can be trusted. Paul said, "Stand firm. Let nothing move you. Always give yourselves fully to the work of the Lord" (1 Corinthians 15:58).

The Christian calling and commitment Since the research makes it quite clear that leadership skill does not result primarily from inborn personality traits, the logical conclusion is that leadership can be learned. This is true. But don't attend a leadership seminar with the expectation of learning to influence your group in the same manner as a skilled platform personality. The confidence and enthusiasm needed to keep a small group interested and spiritually responsive week after week can't be displayed as a learned technique.

The demands on a leader are great and constant. It takes a deep sense of calling and dependence on the Holy Spirit's guidance to sustain the feeling of new challenge and expectation of results every time the group meets. The joy of being in partnership with Jesus makes every lesson exciting and gives the teacher energy to share the excitement, so the group responds, not only to the leader, but also to the evident presence of the Lord.

> **EVALUATE** Go back and consider the ideal leadership traits
> discussed. How do you think members of your group would rate
> you on each? In which area do you most need to improve?

Theories and Applications

Most theories are developed in attempts to answer the question, "What makes a leader effective?" Three approaches are helpful in a study of Christian leadership:

1. *The nature of the group*—how the leader feels about people.
2. *The leadership position*—how the leader conceptualizes the position, leadership behavior, and style of leadership.
3. *Relationships*—how group members relate to one another, how interpersonal relationships are developed in groups.

You may be acquainted with three classic theories that illustrate these approaches. A quick review here will help you to apply the concepts of leadership in the group situation and give you a basis for examining your own leadership behavior as a Christian teacher.

How Do You Feel About People? (Theory X and Theory Y)

The best-known study of how assumptions about the nature of people affect leadership is that of Douglas McGregor.[1] It's known as Theory X and Theory Y. McGregor believes that some leaders make what he calls Theory X assumptions about people. That is, they assume that people in general tend to have little interest in achieving broad goals. Most people are interested in immediate satisfactions. They try to avoid work and responsibility. Either they aren't capable of making significant contributions or they prefer to get by as easily as possible. The Theory X leader feels it is necessary to prod, scold, coax, and expend much effort to maintain interest and influence the behavior of group members.

On the other hand, some leaders make Theory Y assumptions about people. They assume people generally enjoy some challenge, like to do meaningful work, and are willing to strive toward goals that make sense in their world. Most people not only accept responsibility, but frequently seek it. Theory Y assumes that most people are capable of making significant contributions. Most people have untapped potential and will commit themselves to causes they value. The Theory Y leader feels it is important to inform and inspire people and give them opportunities to contribute and grow.

The major concept here is that how you perform as a leader may not depend on your personality traits or skills as much as on how you feel about people.

How *do* you feel about people? Almost no one makes Theory X or Theory Y assumptions about everyone all the time. But if you find that you tend to lean one way or the other most of the time, you can try to adjust your thinking. If you tend to distrust people and have mostly negative reactions to their behavior, probably you need to look for some positive qualities, encourage people more, and preach less. If you are too quick to excuse people and think of them as victims, you may need to be a bit more realistic and help them face themselves honestly.

> **EVALUATE**   Describe how you fit in the Theory X or Theory Y continuum of thinking about the people you lead. Does X or Y better describe your attitude toward people? How does this manifest itself in your leadership? Are you surprised at what your actions say about your attitude toward people? What adjustments should you make?

How Do You Feel About Your Position? (Styles of Leadership)
How you act in your group situation is affected also by how you view your position as a leader. Self-awareness is important. The fact that you are the up-front person gives you power over the lives of others, and requires you to consider how you present yourself and how you are perceived by the group. Do you believe a leader must be strong and firm, maintain order, and supply the correct answers to most questions? Or do you think a leader should mediate the process and allow the members to make most of the decisions, suggest their own conclusions?

An example of research relating to this question is the classic study of three styles of group leadership made by Lewin, Lippitt, and White in 1939.[2] Their plan was to have three groups of young boys work on various projects. To one group was assigned an *authoritarian* leader who provided rigid structure and allowed almost no interaction in the group. The second group was given a *democratic* leader who provided structure but encouraged participation in decision-making and interaction among all members and the leader. An adult in the third group modeled the *laissez-faire* style, providing almost no structure or supervision.

After the experience, the boys were examined in relation to their achievement and their attitudes toward the group, the task, and the leader. Results indicated the democratic group was the most productive and expressed the most satisfaction and least feelings of aggression.

Although the results of controlled tests can't be applied directly and completely to real-life situations, we can learn much from this experiment. One conclusion we can draw is that efforts to control behavior too completely may result in aggression rather than obedience. Teachers of children and adolescents may need this bit of information.

Probably you use all three styles in various situations. Sometimes, strict authority is needed to accomplish a purpose. But if you feel you have been too authoritarian or have allowed the group too much freedom, a change may help the students to be happier and get more from the lessons.

How Do You Develop Relationships? (Transactional Analysis)

Eric Berne believed that in early childhood people begin to develop an "ego image," or idea of themselves, in relationship to others.[3] The way a person sees himself is based on his experiences with people and affects all personal development and human relations. In Thomas Harris' book *I'm OK—You're OK*, four basic positions are described:

1. *I'm OK—You're OK*. This is a position of openness and trust. Interaction is friendly and honest.

2. *I'm OK—You're not OK.* In this position people blame others for their problems, are quick to criticize, and act superior.
3. *I'm not OK—You're OK.* This is the position of the depressed person, who may tend to be a martyr and feel victimized.
4. *I'm not OK—You're not OK.* This is the position of the hopeless person who is unable to cope, does not trust people, may be self-destructive, and may be childish and quick-tempered.[4]

Known as *transactional analysis*, this set of theories has practical applications both in interpersonal relations and group counseling. However, to you as a Christian teacher/leader, the most significant aspect of transactional analysis is that it is based on the assumption that how people feel about themselves is always related to their experiences with other people. Personal development is linked to human relationships. And the group situation is one of the few opportunities available for individuals—from infants to the elderly—to have positive experiences with others and in the company of others.

The youngest child can feel "OK" in a beautiful, friendly place where God's love is demonstrated. He can begin what the theorists call the *life script*, or the inner direction for life, with the knowledge that needs are met in Christ, among His people and by His Word. The elderly one—almost at the hopeless, victimized stage, believing no one cares—can find in a Christian group the basis for new belief in God and man.

> **CONTEMPLATE**   Using the four basic positions from I'm OK—You're OK, what can you do to help people in all but the first group deal with issues of judgment, victimization, or hopelessness that will affect the way they (and, therefore, the group) develop relationships?

A Theory of Leadership for Christian Leaders
The central truth of Christianity is that God created man for His own purpose, and He loves His creation and is willing to do whatever is

necessary to carry out His plan. He elected to use human instruments, from the simple task of naming animals, to building a ship, to unifying a nation, to recording His Word, to the incarnation of Christ.

God did not tell all wayward ones to build little boats, nor did He announce from heaven that they should board the ark in order to be saved. God told Noah, and whatever communication was needed was Noah's responsibility. God did not tell each person in some dispersed multitude to gather and form a nation in the Land of Canaan. He told Abraham. God did not whisper commandments in the ears of Israelites. He told Moses. God did not send individual revelations to the Gentiles. He called Saul of Tarsus.

God instituted the principle of leadership. Leadership is needed, according to God's plan, to accomplish a purpose—to get something done. God does not work in a random way. He knows in advance what His purpose is and how He will move to achieve it. He works through people who are guided and empowered by the Holy Spirit. God's will for a human being is, from God's point of view, an assignment given by Him, the Master Leader, to one who will accomplish a certain task, in order to achieve a purpose or goal that has some meaning in His order.

Understanding of leadership among Christians has been impeded by the fact that most work in the field has focused on the leader and techniques of management and control. Effective Christian leadership begins with the focus on people and God's purpose for them. The leadership task is to motivate and guide people in the attainment of Christian goals.

Therefore, the development of leadership behaviors and techniques must be based on the consideration of three aspects, or orientations: people, tasks, and institutional goals. That is, the leader is concerned with the people in the group (group maintenance), the work that must be accomplished (learning from the lesson presentation and group activities), and the purpose of the total operation (the institutional goal, such as soul winning and church growth).

RATE To discover your style of leadership, mark the choice that best completes each of the following sentences:

1. A Christian teacher/leader should
   a. see that students have a pleasant experience.
   b. do a good job of teaching the lesson.
   c. help build the image and reputation of the church.
2. A Christian teacher/leader must
   a. love the students.
   b. know how to teach at the age level.
   c. think of teaching as part of the church's mission.
3. Christian teacher/leader must have
   a. human relations skills.
   b. competence in group presentations.
   c. interest in theology and doctrine.
4. A good attitude for a teacher/leader to express is,
   a. I enjoy helping people.
   b. I feel good when I've done a job well.
   c. The progress of the whole church is my reward.
5. A good teacher/leader thinks of his or her work as
   a. groups of interacting people.
   b. an instrument for teaching the Bible.
   c. an institution that protects and perpetuates the essential values.

Probably you realized at once that all the items are "correct." This is a test with no wrong answers. But as you went through the items for the first time, did you feel that the *a* items were slightly more important? If you did, then you might be considered a people-oriented leader. If you tended to favor *b* items, you may be a task-oriented leader. If *c* was your real preference, you may be a goal-oriented leader.

If you honestly couldn't decide, then your concept of leadership more nearly fits the model suggested here. The function of the teacher/leader is complex. It includes the coordination of all three aspects: personal interest and awareness of people, competence and dependability in teaching tasks, and commitment to the goals of the church as the institution established to carry on Christ's work until He returns.

Summary

The dual focus in this chapter has been on the relationship between teaching and leadership, and the nature of leadership as the universal process by which people meet their needs and work toward achieving goals.

A remarkable correlation exists between the ideal leadership traits suggested by scholars and scriptural descriptions of those characteristics required in the service of God.

A brief examination of some group theories revealed three major concepts, which can be applied to the leadership functions of Christian leaders. The implications are that your actions as a leader depend to a great extent on the following:

1. *How you feel about people.* Do you think it is difficult to get them to respond, or do you think they are willing, perhaps eager, to respond? It is generally concluded that neither assumption is correct at all times. Good leaders usually have high expectations of people, but they are also realistic.

2. *How you feel about the position of leadership.* Should a leader be authoritarian, democratic, or nondirectional with the group? Good leaders find it necessary to use various styles according to the situation, but the evidence is that democratic groups are more satisfied and productive.

3. *Your knowledge of how people relate to one another.* Experiences with people affect the way individuals feel about themselves and others. The group can provide positive experiences in interpersonal relationships.

A theory of leadership for Christians assumes that God instituted the principle of leadership as His means of working through people to accomplish His eternal purposes. Therefore, the teacher/leader has three main concerns: The people who are to be stimulated and guided, the task of teaching God's Word, and the overall goals of the church.

Evaluate Your Understanding

1. Revisit your definition of leadership at the beginning of this chapter. How would you change or improve it after reading this chapter?

2. What happens in informal gatherings when people feel a need for coordination, administration, or problem solving of any type?

3. According to the chapter, what is the difference between teaching and leadership?

4. True or False: Leadership is one of the few universals of human behavior; it is present in all known societies.

5. Name the ideal seven traits and three Christian traits of a leader from this chapter.

6. What three questions give you a basis for examining your own leadership behavior as a Christian teacher? What are Theory X and Theory Y assumptions about people?

7. What are three styles of leadership that demonstrate how the leader feels about his or her position? In the study cited, which was liked most by members of the group?

8. What is the most significant aspect of transactional analysis for Christian teachers and leaders?

Activate

▶ Plan at least one additional way to improve your competence and leadership skills in the coming weeks—sign up for a class, read one of the recommended books, subscribe to—and read—a leadership journal, contact a mentor or join a support group of other like-minded leaders who want to learn from each other.

▶ Good leaders aren't jealous or afraid to share leadership. Write a brief note of thanks and encouragement to other leaders you work with.

▶ Evaluate the leadership style of a leader who has been a role model for you. Which of the ideal traits of leadership does he or she demonstrate? Does he or she show evidence of ascribing to Theory X or Theory Y about people? Is he or she an authoritarian, democratic, or laissez-faire leader? What knowledge does he or she demonstrate about how people in groups develop relationships?

► Rather than focusing solely on techniques of management and control, resolve to focus more on people and God's purpose for them. Remember, your leadership task is to motivate and guide people in the attainment of Christian goals.

7

CHILDREN LEARN AND GROW IN GROUPS

Each group and each youngster is different.
As a leader or coach, you get to know what they need.
MIKE KRZYZEWSKI

"AND WHAT DID YOU LEARN AT SUNDAY SCHOOL TODAY?" the mother asked her preschool child.

"The teacher was mad at us," the child replied.

On that same morning, in another group room, the teacher expressed approval of a child's handwork project. "It's a very good drawing," she told the girl. At home the child announced, "The teacher likes me."

Children always learn. The challenge in education is to make sure they learn what is intended. The lesson content may have reality or meaning for a child only within the circumstances of its presentation. So, the group room atmosphere must be consistent with the aim of the lesson.

Sensitive teachers realize that what they do has the potential of obscuring or illuminating the content. By taking skillful advantage of an immediate group situation, they may help children learn the content and much more. Every kind of learning has an emotional aspect. Since the emotional climate almost always relates to people, being aware of interpersonal relationships—between teacher and children, among the children, and among those in leadership—is a part of teaching.

> **EVALUATE**   What is the emotional climate in your group? How can you improve the interpersonal relationships between teachers and children to improve the emotional climate?

The main purpose of this chapter is to help you adapt principles of group work to children's groups. To do this, you need some understanding of the social behavior and development of children, and how they affect the child's learning and spiritual growth. Teachers of children have a privilege and responsibility almost beyond full comprehension, since children learn rapidly from every human contact and what they learn first can change their lives.

> **CONTEMPLATE**   What teacher had the greatest influence on you as a child? How did he or she impact your life?

Childhood Experiences Do Have Lasting Effects

Sometimes Christians fear that acknowledging the impact of childhood on later life may lead to soft attitudes toward the sins of adulthood. You may have heard it said that emphasizing early experiences will lead people to blame their parents or environment instead of taking responsibility for their own sins and shortcomings.

However, failing to recognize the powerful impact of early social learning is even more dangerous. The point of studying childhood isn't to fix blame or excuse anyone for making wrong choices. Rather it is to help you understand how conditions develop, so you can deal with them effectively at every stage of life. One of the singular strengths of the Sunday school is its ability to influence family members of different age levels simultaneously and to guide them through the crisis times of the entire life span.

Consider, for example, the problem of child abuse. Most people who abuse children have suffered similar treatment in their own childhoods. Christian teachers who know this are in a better position to help the abused—and the abusers—and to work toward the prevention of child abuse in the future.

Early learning determines or substantially influences all later learning in three major areas: the formation of attitudes, ways of interacting with people, and the development of a perceptual set and vocabulary. These areas provide the framework, or *schemata*, to which all other experiences are subject.

The significance of these processes can be understood by thinking of the child's experience in a fragmented household. An attitude of fear and distrust may develop in relation to a father who has abandoned the family. If the mother is depressed, impatient, and distant, the child is deprived of a warm, bonding experience, which will affect future relationships. If there are no close relatives, no vocabulary is learned and no system is developed by which to think and talk of uncles, aunts, and cousins.

Informed teachers take into consideration the probability that lessons and activities will be interpreted in different ways according to the earlier experiences of students of all ages. The unique situation for children's teachers is that they have greater opportunities than others to establish the framework (or provide the *schemata*), shape the attitudes, and prescribe the interaction patterns that influence all future experiences in relation to God, the church, and the Christian life.

> **INVESTIGATE** For each child you teach, make note of one or two issues or struggles he or she may be dealing with. Make a point of familiarizing yourself with the child's background and family so as to better understand the causes of those difficulties and how you might help.

Attitude Formation

As was stated in chapter 3, attitudes are relatively stable feelings directed at objects, persons, or ideas that predispose one to action. For example, you meet certain missionaries. Your experience with them is pleasant. You like them. Your attitude toward missionaries is affected. Your predisposition is to give in the next missionary offering.

Early attitudes develop almost entirely from social contacts. Whether children feel happy, comfortable, and loved in a group probably will have more effect on their destiny than the most profound doctrinal discussion they ever hear. The one most powerful determinant in a person's attitude toward God and the church is early childhood experience. That thought is almost overwhelming, but it is true. The basic beliefs and values that shape a life begin with what people say and do to children.

Therefore, every lesson should have as one of its objectives to stimulate pleasant feelings toward God, the church, and Christian people. As positive attitudes develop, the predisposition is to accept the Bible teaching and respond in accordance with the suggestions of the teacher.

> **CONTEMPLATE**   What are some positive attitudes you'd like to instill in the children? What are some specific ways you could do so?

Ways of Interacting with People

Children who belong to friendly, active groups acquire social skills. They learn to relate and interact naturally and help others to be comfortable in the group. This is a special and rare bonus every good group can offer.

Teens who are selfish, disrespectful, and unaware of the feelings and needs of others; adults who are distrustful of everyone; and people of all ages who feel too shy and isolated—all are products of their failure to learn how to interact with others during childhood. Because the subject of social skills has been generally neglected by both home and school, many people agonize over their inability to make friends, workshops on interpersonal relations are offered for job seekers, visitors feel unwelcome in churches, and Christians are afraid to initiate a conversation or express an opinion.

Gracious hospitality can be modeled in children's groups and taught to children of all ages. Easy, pleasant conversation, courtesy, the effective presentation of opinions and ideas, the ability to make friends, a genuine participation in Christian community—these can and should be outcomes of childhood group experiences.

> **CONTEMPLATE**   How well do the children in your group interact with other people? In what areas do they need to improve? How can you teach and model better social skills?

Development of a Perceptual Set and Vocabulary

Suppose you experience an unexpected happy turn of events, or something you have feared suddenly works out all right. Which of the following would you be more likely to say? "What a lucky break!" or "Praise the Lord!"

It depends on your *perceptual set*, that is, whether you've learned to perceive events as a matter of luck or as the providence of God. Each experience is interpreted in the light of previous experience and described in terms previously learned. Ways of perceiving and the beginnings of a vocabulary to express what is felt usually are acquired in childhood. Interacting with others in a Christian atmosphere gives children an opportunity to form a *schema* for thinking about God, in the same natural way they learn to walk and talk. This mental framework is the foundation for the development of faith. And it is more effective than direct teaching or preaching. It helps children to develop a kind of "spiritual intuition" and a set of expectations. As they look for indications of God's love, they become increasingly able to discern between His voice and the voice of the world.

> **DEMONSTRATE**   When you are struck by a child's exclamation or vocabulary that reflects a way of thinking in conflict with a Christian worldview, pause a moment and help him or her reframe

the perceptual set and words. It's possible the child has never considered that not being rich or a celebrity might be a blessing rather than an injustice or that parents may enforce rules because they love us. You can help reframe the perceptual set of a child who curses, criticizes, or mocks other children.

Room Climate Affects Learning

Respect and Cooperation Among Workers

It is often stated that the primary qualifications for successful teaching are love for the Lord and love for the children. Sometimes overlooked is the fact that Christian love among colleagues also affects the outcome of teaching. The tone or climate in the area where children meet includes spiritual, educational, and social elements. How workers relate to one another can enhance or destroy all of these.

Studies of excellent and poor public schools prove that children can detect a tone or feeling of warmth, apathy, or chill. Teacher morale and how teachers, principal, and staff members relate to one another influence student morale and achievement. This is true even when the students interact directly with no one except their own teacher. In a children's department where several staff members are in evidence, the effect of relationships is indeed great.

The ideal small group system promotes friendship and cooperation among workers through regular meetings, with many opportunities for discussions between and among the various age-level workers. Exchanges of information and ideas and times of praying together are necessary if a church is to have a unified ministry that keeps in view the life span of its students; the preschooler of today is the middle schooler of tomorrow.

Ideally, children's workers themselves are a true group with specific objectives and goals, a strong trust relationship, an openness to discuss issues, and a spontaneous social and spiritual interaction. The serenity, love, and shared satisfaction of ministry give each worker a positive attitude that manifests itself in facial expressions, voice tone, and body language, which communicate with the children.

Workers who feel too pressed and hurried can't provide the atmosphere of a friendly Christian community, so ideally the team includes extra helpers. They may be in-training teachers and/or volunteers from among singles, teens, or seniors group who serve for designated periods on a rotating basis. This makes possible personal attention to the needs of the children, better facilitation of interaction among the children, and a constant demonstration of adult interaction and service. While Bible truth is being taught, the room can be alive with pleasant activity and people smiling and reaching out to one another in helpful ways.

> **COLLABORATE**   Arrange to meet with the other adults and helpers whose involvement influences the tone and environment of your group. Strive to build respect, affection, and cooperation through discussion and group activities. Discuss how to work together to positively influence all of the children under your care. Pray together for the team and the children.

Demonstration of Teaching-Love

The usual concept of loving people and loving souls isn't the only love teachers must experience and demonstrate. There is a special teaching-love. It is a combination of deep respect for human potential, deep respect for knowledge and truth, and irrepressible eagerness to mediate between the two. The essential qualification for teaching children successfully is to respect and appreciate them. Good teachers are awestruck by children's amazing capabilities and delight in learning from them and helping them to learn from one another.

Objective recognition of a child's achievements is one expression of teaching-love. The teacher who told the child, "It's a very good drawing," is an example. The child interpreted respect for her work as an expression of love. Children respond to high expectations. Your belief in them becomes a kind of self-fulfilling prophecy, as they try to live up to your expectations.

> **EVALUATE** Pay attention to your words and actions as you teach children. What expressions of teaching-love did you notice? Challenge yourself to become more aware of opportunities to express this special teaching-love.

Social Development Affects Learning

At this point it should be clear that children learn more from interaction with people than from objects, books, rules, or any "educational" device. Children are active learners, able to process what is experienced so the total lesson becomes a combination of content and personal perceptions. Therefore, teaching is most effective when the teacher is aware of social factors. The objective of this section is to emphasize the social dimension in childhood development.

Knowledge of social development is valuable to teachers for at least three reasons. First, learning is a social experience. Second, knowledge of social development helps you understand the behavior of children so you are better able to manage group room situations. Third, it helps you guide children in their immediate relations with one another and to develop attitudes and skills necessary for their future relationships.

Explanations of developmental stages usually emphasize individual growth patterns, including physical and psychological or personality factors. Some scholars have recognized that no explanation is complete without reference to the social influence involved in all human behavior. One of them is Erik Erikson. As a basis for understanding how children can be helped to develop socially and spiritually within the context of the group, the discussion here borrows Erikson's description of the stages of childhood.[1]

Stages of Social Development

One of Erikson's basic assumptions is that each stage of life is marked by a particular crisis. When people successfully work through a crisis they are ready for the next stage of life, and they have acquired knowledge and confidence to handle similar crises throughout life. The focus here is not on individual personality development, but on the way each crisis involves human relations.

Attachment and Trust

Almost from birth children begin a kind of seeking, reaching out, behavior that indicates their need for response from other people. Social interaction is spontaneous.

The first need a child has, in addition to the basic biological needs, is to relate to someone. Usually the caretaker is the mother and, in normal situations, she responds to the child. Both physical and emotional needs are met by a person, so what the child experiences isn't only personal comfort and security, but also trust in the source person. Usually, by about 8 months of age, the child has formed what is known as *attachment*. This is the primary social success for the child, and on it may depend, to a great extent, the quality of all future relationships with people.

Erikson describes this early stage of childhood as the time when the infant deals with the *crisis of trust versus mistrust*. He constantly faces the threat of his needs not being met; any delay in satisfaction may lead to a fear of abandonment and, eventually, mistrust. On the other hand, from the same experience the child learns to hope. Hope is a strength that helps to overcome fear, and so when needs are met trust is generated.

If the infant's needs meet with frustration or rejection, further attempts at social interaction may be discouraged. The growing child may feel a general mistrust of people, and so develop behavior and personality traits that make it probable that he will be rejected again.

It is extremely important for teachers to understand what happens to children at this stage of their social development. Early rejections result in failure of the child to trust others. Hope begins to fade. This leads to withdrawal, or antisocial behavior, which a teacher then may interpret as refusal to cooperate, or just "being naughty."

Without realizing it, teachers tend to give approval to the child who has been successful in past social experiences and withhold approval from the one who has not made satisfactory attachments. Other children in the group are influenced by the behavior of the teacher, and a general judgmental attitude may develop toward a certain child. The child feels even more rejected by the teacher and more separated from the group. So the problem escalates.

Scolding, shaming, or ignoring the behavior will not change the child. But something can be done. It isn't too late, in most cases, to help the child form an attachment and begin to develop trust. Many children never have opportunities after their initial failure in infancy to form attachments. This is because they are treated differently. One reason childhood experiences are so difficult to overcome is that people develop expectations based on the behavior of the "normal" child. People encourage children to do what is expected of them at certain stages in their development. Most children respond as expected. The appropriate response meets with encouragement.

But suppose a breakdown in the process occurs. A child who as an infant was not encouraged to respond in the generally accepted manner may at a later stage be scolded for not responding. When a child behaves in an antisocial manner, the best first step is to assume that he has not made a satisfactory social attachment.

Instead of calling attention to the behavior, you can help him form attachments within the group. This can happen at any age, if you are willing to accept the child and provide opportunities for trust to be established. The group can help the child to make up for what was not developed earlier. In this ideal environment, a caring adult can work personally, as well as through the group processes, to give the child a new basis for hope and a new foundation on which to build trust in people, and eventually in God.

> **CONTEMPLATE** What are some ways in which you can help children form attachments within the group instead of calling attention to their misbehavior? What children most need this sort of assistance from you? Outline a workable plan to help them form attachments and overcome any distrust they learned early on.

Identity and Role

Along with learning to trust someone and forming attachments, a major phase in childhood social development is the recognition of self as a separate person, with a place in relation to others. By 18 months of age infants can recognize themselves in mirrors, and by the age of 2 they are pushing for recognition as individual persons. At about this point, children begin to manifest the consciousness of independence and dependence that characterizes human life. They like to venture out alone, but not too far. They enjoy showing what they can do for themselves, but they like to know that a familiar person is nearby. Erikson calls the crisis at this stage *autonomy versus shame and doubt*. It is the stage of acting out personal will against restraint, of "Let me do it by myself." Shame and self-doubt come when attempts at autonomy aren't successful.

The group provides opportunities for the children to practice their personal competencies within recognized boundaries. Group activities show that to comply with legitimate authority does not mean giving up legitimate autonomy. Teachers of this age level can begin to teach one of life's most valuable lessons: Individual satisfactions can be attained within the norms of the group.

The children can learn social roles and can understand that relationships have patterns and rules. They learn to be comfortable in their roles, becoming very upset when an expected role structure is not maintained, as in the case of divorce and remarriage.

In modern society, much emphasis is placed on the development of personal identity. But as children grow toward adolescence the relationship between identity and social role becomes more evident. Children who have secure attachments and think of themselves in terms of roles and relationships become more secure as individuals and struggle less with identity during adolescence. They are more independent and confident than those whose attachments are weak or uncertain. Clearly the function of the group at the stage of autonomy versus shame is to provide a place where children can learn to feel competent within a social structure. Those who know they belong and occupy definite roles are well on their way to satisfactory identity formation.

Development of Conscience

By the time children are 3 or 4 years of age they are quite aware of the role they fill in relation to adults. They are conscious of the difference between the sexes. Active and curious, they want to examine other people and see how others do things. This leads them to get into trouble, or to be intrusive, as Erikson calls it.

The crisis he describes at this point is *initiative versus guilt*. Children in this stage act impulsively, on their own, whereas before, almost everything had been initiated by others. Their new initiative brings problems, as they intrude into areas of "No, no!" "Bad!" "Wrong!" Guilt is experienced as they yield to the temptations of forbidden territory. Play and pretend develop rapidly at this age, when children desire to try out other roles. They identify with adults and imitate them. This represents the beginning of the search for purpose, to "be something," in terms of lifework.

If children experience too much disapproval they may feel guilty whenever they try anything new, and healthy initiative will not develop. On the other hand, if they are treated too permissively they may not develop the legitimate sense of guilt that leads to an understanding of conscience.

A specific function of the group now is to provide sharing experiences where children can try out their ideas of right and wrong and use their need to explore in constructive ways. Acting out is a natural and effective way of doing this. In addition to acting out Bible incidents, have them roleplay life situations. Instead of beginning with rules of behavior, have the children express in drama how they feel in certain circumstances and how they think they should behave. This is an important step in the development of self-direction. You can help them learn to recognize the inner voice of conscience as the "No, no!" that keeps them out of trouble.

School Age and Competition

The family is the initial and most influential group, but the first group experience of which many children are sharply aware is school. Erikson calls the crisis of the school age *industry versus inferiority*.

Children are naturally industrious at this age, but if their attempts at achievement seem to fail, a sense of inferiority can result. Children may feel inferior because a task is too difficult for them. Usually this is because they are judged, or judge themselves, in comparison with others. They may become discouraged and abandon attempts to achieve, causing them to be labeled as slow or disinterested. Then teachers scold them or treat them as slow learners, and they fall even further behind.

There are negative effects too for children who receive praise in comparison with others. They may believe that being ahead is the only worthwhile goal. They try to work out a formula to please the teacher and never allow themselves to be original or creative. So, comparison with others, whether favorable or unfavorable, may lead children to place too much importance on comparisons. As a result, they may fail to appreciate and develop their own unique abilities and contributions.

Thus, the crisis for school children is more social than developmental. It is an irony to hear naive adults tell children to be themselves and not compare themselves with others. The social system in general—and group room situations in particular—require, even force, children to compare, contrast, and judge themselves in relation to the characteristics and achievements of others.

Although there is a trend toward less emphasis on competing, competition is prevalent enough in modern life that many children may never experience true group cohesiveness unless the church provides the opportunity. In some homes, both parents have outside employment and talk freely of competition at the workplace. Perhaps active rivalry exists even between the parents themselves, resulting in separation, divorce, or bickering. The children are urged to compete at school and in sports. Television constantly gives messages of competition among products, contestants, political rivals, and athletes. It may seem to children that all human relations are competitive.

Teachers and leaders of school-age children must make sure the church provides a group experience as free as possible from competition. Plan some joint projects, with opportunities for numerous types of contributions. Make "jigsaw" assignments, so that a project is complete only when each child supplies a component. Emphasize the positive aspects of the division of labor. Have the group make a chart showing all the offices and functions of the church. Explain how these relate and interact. Point out the connection group members have to the church and its national and worldwide ministries. Show that every person and every type of work has a place.

Next to an experience with Christ, school-age children need most to learn how to interact with love and trust, to respect people, and to appreciate a variety of personalities, achievements, and contributions. They can learn this best in a Christian group environment. Where Christ is Lord, everyone is important, and there is no thought of anyone winning or losing.

> **RESTATE**   Fill in the chart with the appropriate information according to Erikson's teaching about the stages of social development. You may wish to test your understanding and memory before looking back at the text to verify that your answers are correct.

STAGE OF DEVELOPMENT	APPROXIMATE AGE	CRISIS	FUNCTION OF THE GROUP
Attachment and trust			
Identity and role			
Development of conscience			
School age and competition			

Summary

This chapter has explained how principles of group work apply to children's groups. The central theme has been that learning is a social experience. Especially for children, the social climate of the group room and the attitudes and behaviors of the staff members become part of the lesson. Knowledge of childhood social development helps teachers to understand children's behavior and to use group functions and processes to full advantage at each stage.

Early learning determines or substantially influences all later learning in three major ways.

1. Children form attitudes that may permanently affect the way they think and feel about people and ideas.
2. Children learn ways of interacting with people.
3. Children develop perceptual sets and vocabulary that determine how they will perceive and describe future experiences.

Group room climate, including the way workers interact with one another, affects the learning experiences of children. The most effective teaching is done by those who respect children, acknowledging their abilities and potential, and express high expectations for them.

Erik Erikson's explanation of the stages of human development shows that each stage involves social interaction. The goal of social development is a healthy understanding and acceptance of dependence and independence. The group provides the ideal environment for helping children to grow as loving, sharing Christians, secure in their own ability to contribute and appreciative of the contributions of others.

Evaluate Your Understanding

1. What is and what is not the point of studying childhood for the Christian leader?
2. According to this chapter, what's one of the singular strengths of the Sunday school as it relates to families?

3. Early learning determines or substantially influences all later learning in what three major areas?
4. What is a perceptual set and how does it impact a person's vocabulary? Give one example.
5. How workers relate to one another can enhance or destroy the tone or climate in what three areas?
6. How does the ideal Christian small group system promote friendship and cooperation among workers?
7. According to this chapter, what is teaching love as it relates to children?
8. Knowledge of the stages of social development is valuable to teachers for at least what three reasons?
9. Describe what young children experience during the crisis of trust versus mistrust.
10. When a child behaves in an antisocial manner, the best first step is to assume what?

Activate

▶ Read a book on child development geared specifically toward the age group you teach.
▶ Provide safe and loving opportunities for children to create attachments and learn to trust.
▶ Consider children who have caused problems in the past in a different light based on your learning from this chapter. Pray for them and attempt to meet their true needs.
▶ Remember, children are tuned in to your tone, facial expressions, body language, and words used. Be careful not to allow damaging negative feelings to seep out when you are tired, busy, or distracted.
▶ Schedule a visit with each child—in his or her home, if possible—so you can better understand his or her needs and situation.

8

ADOLESCENCE CAN BE DEFINED AS RELATIONSHIPS

*Don't laugh at a youth for his affectations. He is only
trying on one face after another to find his own.*
LOGAN PEARSALL SMITH

"MY BOYFRIEND IS 16. He asked me to have sex with him. I told him I wasn't sure if I was ready yet. I'm afraid to tell my mother about this. How do I know when I'm ready? Please answer soon, because there are many others who need to know."

This comes from a question written by a 14-year-old girl to an advice columnist. The words and circumstances can be understood to indicate the following:

1. According to modern custom, teenage sex is a normal, open subject to be discussed.
2. Young people are ready to accept what seems to be normal in society, but they have some uncertainties. They need to test their own feelings. They reach out for advice.

3. The home can't be depended on to provide instruction and guidance. There may be no honest, trusting relationship, no warm feeling of acceptance and understanding, between the teen and his parents.
4. Young people are afraid of being scolded, rejected, and put down. They may be willing to accept advice, but they aren't willing to subject themselves to arbitrary treatment.
5. The basic "teen problem" isn't sex, or rebellion, so much as it is the failure of adults to provide appropriate teaching and communication.

The question raises another question: Where are the Christian leaders?

This girl's question and the widespread conditions from which it results relay a distressing message: Teens who want information and advice may find a total stranger more friendly and credible than anyone at home or in the church.

> **INVESTIGATE**   If you have never done so, go online and search for teen advice columns to see the sorts of questions today's teens are asking. You may be shocked—and even more so by the answers they are receiving on these sites.

The church tends to make two serious mistakes in dealing with adolescents. First, in most situations, they are treated as an audience, rather than a group. Therefore, they don't learn to interact freely and develop a comfortable sense of belonging, appreciation, and trust among peers and leaders. They are treated more as objects of evangelism than as actual or presumed-to-become members of the Body.

Second, teens' search for identity, personal fulfillment, and confirmation of ideology is interpreted as rebellion or rejection of established values. This leads them to become defensive or to feel confused and uncertain about their relationship with the church.

These mistakes result in part from Christian leaders' acceptance of stereotypes of adolescence. In their zeal to keep young people in church, many leaders overreact. They over control and try to manipulate teenagers. Others use high-energy programs in an effort to control rather than actually try to understand the nature of adolescent growth or study the stages of mental, moral, and social development.

If they really tried, these leaders would discover that at the very time it seems most difficult to keep youth involved in church, many teens' favorite social activity is "hanging out" with a group of their peers. They gather more or less regularly, just to be together. Although they seem to have no structure or purpose, they are meeting for the same reasons people generally join and maintain groups. They need interaction. They seek information from one another. They test their feelings and ideas. They look for meaning, and they develop relationships.

Probably a church group will never be accepted by teens as their favorite place to hang out. But if it is designed as a group activity, by people who understand and try to meet teens' real needs, the young people will sense it, and attendance is likely to be good.

The main purpose of this chapter is to help you to lead such a group. The first step is to understand the problems associated with adolescence and to realize the group's potential power to make significant differences in the lives of teens. You will then be able to evaluate and adapt your leadership style, as you find appropriate, and guide the group in developing and maintaining the Christian support group they require.

If you teach children, material concerning adolescence is relevant, since most teens' problems have their roots in childhood, and the best treatment for any problem is prevention. If you teach adults, your knowledge of adolescence is still invaluable. You will better understand many of the problems of young marrieds, be able to help the parents of teenagers, or help to bring about good relationships between teens and their grandparents.

> **RATE** What teacher or leader had the biggest impact on your life when you were the age of your group members? Explain what

made them effective and memorable. What can you learn from their example to help you make a difference in the lives of your teens?

Looking Behind the Visible Problems

CONTEMPLATE Make a list of the biggest problems you see facing young people in your nation, community, and group. Now make a list of what you believe are the best answers to those problems. What are you doing to help teens in these areas?

In 2015, the Centers for Disease Control and Prevention (CDC) reported a total of 229,715 babies were born to women ages 15–19 years, for a birth rate of 22.3 per 1,000 women in this age group. This is another record low for U.S. teens and a drop of 8 percent from 2014. However, the teen pregnancy rate in the United States is substantially higher than in other western industrialized nations.

People are most likely to begin abusing drugs during adolescence and young adulthood. By senior year, 70 percent of high schoolers have tried alcohol, 50 percent have tried an illegal drug, 40 percent have smoked a cigarette and approximately 20 percent will have used a prescription drug for a non-medical purpose, according to the National Institute on Drug Abuse.

The frequency and seriousness of delinquent acts are increasing. The suicide rates for adolescent boys and girls have been steadily rising since 2007, according to the CDC. The suicide rate for girls ages 15 to 19 doubled from 2007 to 2015, when it reached its highest point in 40 years. The suicide rate for boys ages 15 to 19 increased by 30 percent over the same time period. Suicide is the second or third major cause of death among teens. A marked increase has occurred in eating disorders (anorexia nervosa, self-starvation; and bulimia, binge eating followed by self-induced vomiting).

Statistics change so rapidly that specific numbers are of little value. The point is, you are faced almost every day with reports of the major problems of adolescence: sex, drugs, delinquency, eating disorders, and suicide. It is understandable if you perceive adolescence as a time of turmoil and danger. Your reaction may be to cry out against sin and warn young people about the evils of modern life.

But did you ever consider asking why a certain percentage of teens aren't involved in the statistics? Some very good studies have been made from this viewpoint. They are called *correlational studies*, since the methodology is to find out if some variables (that is, conditions or characteristics) generally go together. For example, a correlation exists between the number of babies born in a community and the number of diapers sold in the nearest shopping center. Although this does not prove a cause-and-effect relationship, there is some significance here for those who might seek a location for the distribution of diapers!

Correlational studies show that the variables that correlate most consistently with avoidance of drug and alcohol abuse, teenage sexual activity, eating disorders, delinquency, and teenage suicide are relationships with adults and stable institutions such as the home, the church, and the school. Those who are most involved in family, church, and school activities are least likely to be affected by the teenage problems. Those who are most detached from home, church, and school are most likely to be involved in such problems.

This isn't to suggest that the complex and painful conditions experienced by any individual can be explained or resolved easily. However, it may help you to see a brief summary of explanations generally given in regard to the major conditions treated in textbooks on adolescence.

Sexual Behavior

The adolescent's physical development makes it natural that he is acutely aware of sex. Treatment of sex in the media is a powerful influence. Sex outside marriage is the normal and expected behavior in most cases. The notion of romance in the culture makes it okay to be "in love," whereas objective approaches to relationships are rejected.

Conventional sex education in the schools and the availability of birth control may be somewhat effective in deterring pregnancies.

Modeling in the home is a *highly significant factor*. Most researchers agree that open communication, early teaching, and healthy relationships with family members, friends, and concerned adults are the best means of dealing with the issue.

> **INVESTIGATE**   Check out the television programs, movies, music, and video games popular with members of your group. What is being taught about sexual behavior? About drugs and alcohol? About acceptable behavior, eating disorders, suicide, social media, families, God, and the church? Don't be afraid to talk about what they're seeing and hearing to help them make sense of things from a biblical perspective.

Drug and Alcohol Abuse

Teens experiment with drugs and alcohol mostly out of curiosity. Almost all substance abuse occurs in a social situation. Peer pressure is strong, but the influence of the home can determine the degree to which teens respond to peer pressure. The presence of alcohol and other drugs in the home, and modeling by the parents, are significant variables in the use of these substances.

Substance abuse almost always is correlated with other problems. That is to say, happy, healthy young people who have hope and direction in life aren't suddenly carried away by drugs. Attachment to a group with an ideological or religious cause probably is the most effective deterrent to substance abuse.

> **RELATE**   When a celebrity enters rehab or overdoses on drugs, use it as a learning opportunity for your adolescents. What are some of the pitfalls of fame? Should such people be idolized? Is illegal drug use ever safe and acceptable?

Delinquency

Testing the limits of control and trying to "beat the system" seem to be part of growing up. Traffic violations and minor lawbreaking are common among young people of every socioeconomic group, family background, and religious faith. But serious delinquency results from failure to internalize or accept the values of society.

Some delinquency can be partially explained by feelings of being cheated, or left out economically, by society, as is the case with chronically unemployed youth. But often delinquency results because teens feel left out in other ways. They see no reason to care about their parents' values. They feel no obligation or loyalty to any segment of society. Morality is tied to social affiliation and to trust in the honesty and reliability of the group. Discovery of what they perceive to be hypocrisy and deception seriously shakes the faith of teens and may lead to cynicism about their elders' rules and laws.

Eating Disorders

Adolescent girls are made very aware of cultural measures of attractiveness. To be thin is in. They may hear their mothers talk of dieting, and even insist that they diet. They may be teased at home about their weight. Almost all experiment with dieting.

However, serious eating problems, like drug problems, are symptoms of other conditions; they are without physical explanation. For example, those who treat anorexics believe it is a family disease. It indicates failure to adapt, or to receive the satisfaction and care needed. Sometimes it is a bid for attention. The most successful treatment seems to be that which helps the anorexic develop personal identity through satisfying relationships with family and peers, rather than through self-starvation.

Suicide

Almost all adolescent suicides occur after a long series of negative experiences. Perhaps the young person never fully developed the sense of trust and hope necessary for normal growth. Family problems and breakdowns in communication almost always are involved. In the notes teens leave, they often indicate they have been considering suicide for a considerable period of time. They have tried to cope with problems, but have run into constant barriers and disappointments, and now can see no other way out.

Suicide has long been considered a social rather than an individual problem, in that almost all cases relate to the inability to find satisfactory relationships with others. Almost always there are warning signs, such as talk of suicide, obvious depression, and withdrawal. Some scholars believe that most teenage suicides are cries for attention and love from adults, and that many of them could be prevented if warning signs were heeded.

Identity and Resocialization

Since people are born into an established set of human relationships and behavioral expectations (that is, ways of doing things, or culture), their first task is to fit in. They learn what is expected of them and adapt to the situation as they find it.

This is what is meant by *socialization*. If everything were to go smoothly, people's needs all would be met and they would be received as members of society, with no questions or doubts on either side. They would grow up, fully accepting all the ready-made ways. Thinking and decision-making would be practically unnecessary.

No one really desires such a condition. Almost everyone appreciates to some degree the imagination and creativity of youth, the willingness to question some established customs and values, the courage to fight injustice, the eagerness to generate ideas and produce inventions.

The transition between original socialization (or fitting in and becoming accepted) and eventual mature, contributing membership in society is what's known as *the search for identity*. In general, the goal of adolescence isn't a rejection of society but a kind of resocialization. Teens are no longer taken-for-granted infants but specific, individual personalities. They don't wish to disassociate but to have a voice in how they will associate. They need to perceive themselves as unique beings, yet they wish to maintain a feeling of continuity with the past and a meaningful relationship with a social unit whose values they can accept as their own.

Almost without exception, teens desire to commit themselves on the basis of their own decisions to an ideology or value system. What they perceive as identity includes their own special relationship to a reference group.

At their stage of development, adolescents have not acquired the ability to think through complex situations and anticipate consequences. Their thinking tends to be egocentric; that is, they make very personal applications. They are emotionally involved with the immediate implications of whatever is said or done. Impatient to establish their own position, they reject some of the ideas and values of their elders.

Often the elders react too quickly, failing to notice just what has been rejected. Usually, in the beginning, only relatively superficial matters are involved—such as music and dress. Adults who are acquainted with the process of identity formation can provide understanding and guidance. In most cases, people later return to the basic philosophies, political positions, and religious beliefs that influenced them in childhood.

The Process of Identity Formation

Again, the work of Erikson can be called upon to provide some insights.[1] He suggests four possible outcomes in the process of identity formation. First is the possibility of *foreclosure*. This is premature identity formation, resulting frequently from lack of opportunity for personal development. The young person feels coerced, or for some reason is unable to make individual choices. He accepts ready-made ideas and values and never becomes truly mature in thinking and experience.

Forcing and shaming children in regard to religious decisions lead to this condition and deprive the person of a mature Christian experience. Adolescents should be taught that it is normal to review their earlier experiences and make new commitments to Christ on the basis of their greater understanding as young adults. As resocialization is to relationships in society, so is new commitment in relation to Christianity. To an adolescent, being a Christian means something different from what it did when he was a child, because he has become a different person. Foreclosure in Christian experience can lead to lifelong spiritual immaturity.

The second possibility is *identity confusion*. It results when adolescents experience extreme tensions, such as might occur when they want to accept the values of their parents as well as those of their peer group, or when they get mixed signals, such as when they see parents and teachers not living by the values they verbalize.

Children who have been neglected, abused, abandoned, or exposed to broken or unhappy homes have difficulty in identity formation. Those who have never been taught systematically or given a foundation for development of values find it difficult to commit themselves to any value system. Such persons tend to be indifferent to goals and uncertain about their futures.

Open discussion in a Christian group can help these young people clarify their thinking. They need the support of a caring, listening adult who expresses confidence and joy, models Christianity, and shows real interest in helping young people develop their potential.

Negative identity is a possible outcome when adolescents feel too much pressure. Autocratic parents; strict, impersonal supervision; and being forced into activities in which they have no interest may lead teens to do exactly the opposite of what is expected of them. Usually they are being vindictive and acting out their hurts, and in reality, are uncomfortable with such behavior.

Rebellious actions; negative, argumentative attitudes; using drugs; running away; even becoming pregnant—these are some indications of negative identity formation. Since much of what they do is pretense (at least in the beginning), loving them and being patient with them can be marvelously effective. These adolescents can't be forced or shamed, but often they are among the most ready to respond when they understand God's grace. They need to be accepted as they are; this is what is meant by grace.

The fourth possibility is what Erikson calls a *moratorium*. Instead of developing a mature identity and making strong commitments, some adolescents seem to prefer to drift for a while and look over their options. They may go on trips or try out a different life alone in the city. This behavior isn't always a cause for great concern. It can be constructive, if it is not allowed to continue until it becomes habitual.

The role of the church in such cases isn't to condemn, but to try to keep in touch and help the young person find ways of using his experiences as bridges to mature decisions.

> **EVALUATE**   For each possible outcome in the process of identity formation, describe the causes, the signs, any group members who fit this category, and possible ways to help these young people have a positive outcome.

POSSIBLE OUTCOME	CAUSES	SIGNS	GROUP MEMBERS	STRATEGIES FOR HELPING
Foreclosure				
Identity Confusion				
Negative Identity				
Moratorium				

The Group as an Agency for Socialization

This brief overview of adolescents' problems and needs should lead you to conclude that the church's most effective strategy is to ensure that teens are firmly attached to the Body as a social institution as well as the center of their religion. Experience has proven that neither conventional evangelistic efforts alone, nor programs of Christian entertainment and social events fully accomplish this purpose. What is required is patient, loving socialization or incorporation of teenagers into the church body. For this, the small group is ideal.

1. Remember the question asked of the advice columnist? Teenagers actively seek information. Set forth Bible content as information about people with problems, making mistakes

and finding answers. Make direct application to the spiritual, emotional, and social needs of the group. But instead of sermonizing or pointing out "lessons," give frequent opportunities for questioning and clarifying possible misunderstandings. Ask them if they see applications.

2. Give teens many opportunities to talk about spiritual experiences and to express doubts and failures. Provide an atmosphere of friendly peers where any idea can be shared and any question asked, without pressure or embarrassment.

3. Give many opportunities to make new commitments to the Lord, without pressure, as natural expressions of developing insights.

4. Be willing to accept the calling (which means to expend the energy and time necessary) to be the type of caring and competent adult every teen needs from time to time. Provide direction and example. Be an approachable, available, mature Christian friend.

5. Guide the group in the development of norms. Help them provide cues for behavior, standards, and models among peers. Remember, peer pressure works in church too.

6. Encourage conversation and sharing of experiences that will lead group members to respect one another and to appreciate personal differences, talents, and abilities.

7. Provide many opportunities for group members to contribute and to develop individuality in accepted ways. Let them exercise leadership skills, learn to give and receive approval graciously, and experience success in cooperation rather than in competition.

8. Make the group a place where people show compassion and serve others, not only in directed projects, but also in spontaneous activities.

The Teacher/Leader
Teachers of adolescents are most effective when they assume a leadership role that goes beyond presiding over a group on Sunday or

weekday night. Since the primary task of the church in regard to its young is to get them attached to the Body, the teacher must be very obviously and vocally attached. He/she must be able and willing to interact with other teachers and youth workers and make every effort to synchronize group activities with other youth activities. For example, cooperative activities could be planned for celebrating graduation or hosting a special youth speaker.

> **CONTEMPLATE**   Think of an upcoming church-wide event. How can your teens be involved? How can you help them to be comfortable participants?

The basic qualities of deep spiritual commitment, competence in Bible teaching, and sincere respect for people are indispensable for those who work with adolescents. In addition, youth leaders must be emotionally mature, secure and trusting, not too self-conscious, and able to exercise consistent, natural authority. Neither "being pals" nor being arbitrary and autocratic is acceptable to young people.

Young people respond to many styles of leadership. Leaders may be young or nearing old age. They may bubble over with good humor or speak with quiet wisdom. But they all must be genuine. Characteristics in leadership most likely to be rejected are self-righteousness, heavy-handed coaching (or "motivational" tactics), and talking down (or otherwise causing the young people to feel like they're being treated like children).

Adolescents seem to prefer leaders who are willing to share their own experiences, disclose their own problems and weaknesses, and yet demonstrate competence and victory.

This reflects the general tendency of people to like those who are competent, but also vulnerable. This was shown in one rather whimsical experiment, where subjects were asked to express their preference among three persons who answered difficult questions. One had answered with near perfection. One was less proficient. One had answered with near perfection, but had spilled his coffee during the questioning. The winner by a significant margin was the near-perfect scholar who spilled coffee! It is fine to be very knowledgeable, but to be perfect is too much.

Summary

The key to adolescent conflict and struggle is a desire to belong versus a desire to be an individual. That is why teens will rebel against parents, yet conform in peer groups. Usually they aren't rebelling so much as expressing their need for freedom and individuality. What they perceive as identity is closely related to identification with a group whose values they can claim as their own.

The task of the church is to guide adolescents in forming satisfying relationships within the body of Christ. Good churches appreciate the potential of teenagers and help them meet their needs for identity, self-expression, and social interaction, without breaking away from Christian values. The small group provides the ideal combination of teaching, group forces, and interaction with peers and adult leaders who model the basic concepts of identity and fulfillment in Christ.

Evaluate Your Understanding

1. What two serious mistakes does the Christian world tend to make when dealing with teens?
2. Why do Christian leaders make these mistakes with teens?
3. What are some of the reasons adolescents want to be part of a group?
4. What are the first steps in making your group an appealing opportunity that meets teens' needs?
5. What are correlational studies?
6. What variables do studies show us are most closely linked with avoiding risky teen behaviors?
7. Why do so many teens break the rules?
8. What causes serious delinquency?
9. Why do some teens reject morality

10. What are the four possible outcomes in the process of identify formation as described by Erickson?

Activate

▶ Consider setting up your own advice column for your group. Allow young people to write or post questions confidentially and answer them (in an online forum or when your group meets).

▶ Allow plenty of time for unstructured interacting and just hanging out together in your group.

▶ Meet with other leaders of teens to brainstorm strategies and activities, encourage, and pray with each other.

▶ Review the material in this chapter and pray specifically for each group member.

9

MATURE CHRISTIANS WORK TOGETHER

If your actions inspire others to dream more, learn more,
do more and become more, you are a leader.

JOHN QUINCY ADAMS

THERE WAS A TIME when the admonition "Act your age" had meaning. Certain behaviors were considered normal at particular periods of life, and social approval was given or withheld on the basis of these accepted stages.

But times (or rather social conditions) have changed. A grandmother may be a 35-year-old who plays professional tennis. A 65-year-old couple starts out to seek adventure in a new RV. A 70-year-old father attends graduate school with his son. One woman may be getting her first job at 50, while her neighbor of the same age is taking early retirement. Mothers are in the teen group at church, and grandfathers in the college and career group.

People don't fit into neat packages. The church is faced with the exciting challenge of recognizing rapid social change and planning Bible-teaching programs to meet emerging needs. Adult groups must be viewed as social groups—heterogeneous, interacting—with members influencing one another perhaps as much as they are influenced by the teacher.

Your adult group is a group of interesting people with active, inquiring minds. Most of them adapt to life in marvelously creative ways and have treasures of experience to share. Probably some would like to be friendlier and more involved, but they don't know how. With your knowledge of the social nature of people and the group processes, you can help them. This will make the group more stimulating for you as well as the members.

The main purpose of this chapter is to apply group work principles to adults in the church's small groups. In a generalized view of the adult life span, we will consider factors common to both singles and married people. The brief examination of three stages of adult social development is loosely based on the group classifications suggested by Erikson.

The discussion of group processes and leadership has a dual objective: to enhance your own leadership skills and to help you teach the adults how to use their various talents and interests in church leadership positions and interpersonal relations. This will benefit the entire church as an organization and a body.

> **MOTIVATE** What budding skills, talents, and propensities have you observed in the members of your group? Recognizing the potential is an important first step. What can you do to encourage and motivate these individuals to grow and move forward in the gifts God has given them to share with others?

Adult Stages of Social Development

Erikson divides the adult life span into three major stages.[1] He describes each stage in terms of the type of adjustment a person commonly makes at that point in life. This may be called a crisis since usually a person must make some choices that will affect the rest of his life. (The term *crisis* does not refer to a serious emotional problem, but to some marked change, usually involving interpersonal relationships).

Young Adulthood—Intimacy Verses Isolation

The main characteristic of young adulthood is that it is a time of making life-shaping decisions about marriage, parenthood, career, and other significant attachments. Commitments might be made tentatively during the teenage period, but now sure choices are required.

In a society where individuality and privacy are valued, the young adult experiences tension. How much of self can be relinquished in order to enjoy the stability and comfort of intimate relationships? On the other hand, refusal to make commitments can lead to aimless, self-centered loneliness.

The term *intimacy versus isolation* expresses this tension between forming relationships and pulling away from people and social obligations. The development of both mature love and ethics depends to a great extent on one's ability and willingness to overcome self-interest and fear of rejection so that appropriate relationships can be formed. The word *intimacy* is used to mean binding, close associations that require some self-sacrifice. Although the model for intimacy is marriage, the ability to relate intimately to others isn't exclusive to marriage. Devotion, dedication, self-sacrifice, and ethical behavior are required in relationships with children, parents, friends, associates, and affiliations with various services and ministries.

If the person has learned moral obligation (that is, obedience) during childhood and has been able to establish his identity and make serious commitments during adolescence, he has a foundation for the intimacy and commitment required in mature love. Out of love comes the development of respect for people and the compulsion to be ethical in all interpersonal contacts. The healthy individual at this stage can risk being intimate and is trustworthy and dependable in all types of relationships. Adulthood is reached when the individual is ready to relinquish to a great extent the role of being cared for and to take on the responsibility of nourishing and caring for others.

> **CONTEMPLATE**   What made you first feel like an adult? How does that compare to what the above paragraph says about the mark of adulthood?

> **COLLABORATE**   You may wish to brainstorm with your group responses to the following open-ended sentences: "I knew I was an adult when I...," "Being an adult means...," and "The hardest/best part about being an adult is..." Discuss what this chapter says about the necessity of putting aside self-interest and fear of rejection to love and care for others as being hallmarks of healthy adulthood.

If moral obligation and an adequate sense of identity have not been developed, this can be a stage of isolation. The individual is afraid to risk relationships and may wish to avoid contacts and commitments. He may be so unwilling to compromise his own position that he never learns how to enjoy interaction and love.

Modern society may encourage isolation, considering self-interest a value and emphasizing avoiding being exploited by others. An example of this is a model marriage contract that makes legal provision for the division of assets and responsibilities during marriage and ensures the rights of each party in case of divorce. Today's young women may experience serious stress in deciding how to balance intimacy with isolation. Feminism has sometimes exaggerated the need for women to be assertive and wary of putting themselves under obligation to others.

The Christian group has a critical function at this stage when many young adults are torn between intimacy and isolation, between a desire to affiliate and a fear of commitment. The group can demonstrate what the teacher proclaims—that there are stable values. People who love and trust one another can work toward shared goals without destroying anyone's individuality. In the Christian body, the relationship between giving and receiving is forever settled. Those who are willing to lose their lives in the Christian sense find them in new abundance. And love that is willing to sacrifice is the only hope of life.

Maturity—Generativity Versus Stagnation

Most treatments of adult life include a listing of various crises, or transition points. At about age 30, people often undergo a period of reevaluation. They are more likely to go back to school or to make career changes. At about 45 to 50, they may experience a midlife crisis, pondering the meaning of life and deciding how the remainder of their lives will be spent.

How each individual is affected by these critical life changes depends almost entirely on the situation, especially whether the person has satisfying relationships and meaningful activity.

Research shows that people who are interested and involved in the development and progress of their social and institutional surroundings express more satisfaction with life and suffer fewer negative consequences of change than those who are preoccupied with their own feelings and conditions. Assumption of responsibilities, voluntary public service, acts of altruism, and expressions of interest and anticipation about the future are characteristic of those who have emotional health and maturity.

> **ORCHESTRATE** Look around you. What needs do you see in your community, neighborhood, or church? Involve group members in planning opportunities for public service, acts of altruism, and the assumption of responsibilities for an important cause. There is no better way to turn people's attention from themselves to interest in others and anticipation about the future.

These facts lead to the conclusion that the most significant concept of adult life is not crises or developmental stages, but *generativity*. The term indicates a concern with establishing and guiding the next generation, desiring to pass on something of oneself to the future.

In a broader sense, generativity refers to the need of the mature person to be needed, to make contributions to others now, and to do something of lasting consequence. It includes much more than physical procreation. Every mature person has a desire to create and produce. Generativity is the driving force that ensures continuity of life and institutions. It includes a compulsion to teach. Ultimately, of course, this reflects man's purpose in the plan of God. From this point of view, the ministry of the group leader always is twofold: to lead and to prepare others to lead.

It is possible that God works with His created beings according to cultural and social changes. Whatever the case, today is marked by a tremendous emphasis on a kind of religious activity compatible with the electronic media and modern tastes for the dramatic. The explosive, miraculous, charismatic programs of super churches and super personalities have a powerful influence over the way Christian ministry is perceived and conducted. Certainly, every Christian can rejoice that the secular world is being bombarded with the gospel, and the influence of the Pentecostal movement has never been so potent.

In this loud moment for the church, however, take time to think about the need for a quiet, stable leader: one whose hope transcends the immediate excitement; one who is committed to preserve and perpetuate the truth if Jesus tarries, to plant and water and gently nourish attitudes and expectations for tomorrow's harvest. That's generativity. The leader who recognizes and cultivates this quality meets not only a short-term need of older adults, but also a long-term need of the church—a need essential to sustaining the church in its comprehensive ministry of worship, evangelism, teaching, and compassion.

> **CONTEMPLATE**   Look at the description of a stable leader in the paragraph above. How do you rate when you compare yourself to this? How do you demonstrate these traits? How can you improve to better accomplish your mission of leading others to fulfill the church's comprehensive ministry of worship, evangelism, teaching, and compassion?

The opposite of generativity is stagnation: when adults are allowed to feel useless and unnecessary. Such a condition can blight both the church of today and the church of tomorrow. The attitude of stagnation isn't so much a sin of the congregation as it is a by-product of a certain type of church program. At the stage in life when mature adults most need to generate life and nourish others, many of them seem content to sit quietly, anonymously, and partake as children drinking milk. They seem inclined to avoid involvement and keep themselves free to enjoy their own interests.

But deep within most mature adults is a latent desire, perhaps even unconscious, to contribute something that will outlast their own lives. Their stagnation results from a lack of stimulation and teaching more often than from personal apathy or unconcern.

No one is in a better position than an enlightened and concerned group leader to discover and enlist latent talents, stir people out of complacency and self-interest, and guide them into lively participation.

> **CONTEMPLATE**   Now consider the members of your group. Which word better describes them—generativity or stagnation? What latent talents or potential do you see in each? What practical steps can you take to stir people out of complacency and self-interest and guide them into lively participation?

Later Adulthood—Integrity and Wisdom Versus Despair

The most beautiful and revealing example of God's creation is an elderly Christian. Nothing on earth is so magnificent as a mature, loving, wise, confident, and complete human being. He is sure that life has been worth whatever it has cost and is eager to continue, but is also ready to experience the transition. Such a person is living and loving all the way to heaven.

The critical issue in later adulthood is a tension between integrity and despair. As people age, they may accept and enjoy their strong position of having accomplished the major tasks of life. Integrity implies a process of integration in which experiences of the past are blended with the present and future. Individuals with integrity realize they are part of an ongoing process. They are grateful to those who contributed to their lives. They are eager to accept responsibility in the present. They are willing to release leadership roles to the younger generation at an appropriate time. This ability to utilize accumulated knowledge and experience and to put oneself into perspective in relationship to others is the true wisdom of maturity.

Those who do not develop integrity tend to look back with regrets. They are anxious and despairing because time is passing so rapidly. They may try to hang on to youth by going to extremes in superficial matters, such as dress and grooming. They may feel hopeless and fatalistic. Or they may be bitter and resentful when younger people take over positions of leadership.

> **EVALUATE**   Based upon the descriptions above, who have you known that has best exemplified an older person with integrity? Who has been the most tragic example of an older adult who has not developed this sort of integrity? Now consider your own life. Which type of person are you becoming?

It's sad to acknowledge that even true practicing Christians can suffer despair instead of victory as they grow older. But being willing to admit it and knowing the basic reason for it are the first steps toward helping such people.

The basic reason is that these individuals have never learned to relate satisfactorily to others. People who have a genuine sense of belonging to the Body do not need the constant reassurance of personal worth. They accept the joys of the Body as their own. But if they were uncertain of their place in the group as adolescents, felt isolated and detached as young adults, and never became responsible contributors in their mature years, it is difficult for them to rejoice in the victory of the group as they grow older. Even so, there is a positive note: People in general are never too old to form and enjoy relationships.

Not long ago, it was common to refer to the *disengagement theory*, which states that older people gradually withdraw from social contact. As roles of parenthood and employment become less important, it was said, their world shrinks. They tend to become inactive and prefer not to be involved.

More recent investigation proves that descriptions of inaction and withdrawal don't fit the majority. Many people begin new careers after retirement. Many develop completely new circles of friends after moving from their homes. Almost all prefer to be active, to mingle with people, to assume authentic responsibilities. If these facts were fully understood and acted upon, it is likely the despair of declining years could be essentially eliminated in a happy Christian community.

Application of Group Principles

The approach used throughout this book is to base Christian group work on an understanding of the nature and needs of people, rather than on methods and instructions. This approach helps you understand the reasons behind the behavior you see so you will be able to adapt your methods to the situation in a more realistic way.

For example, teachers of adults often say that they use the lecture method so much because adults will not participate, or because some individuals abuse the privilege of discussion, monopolize time, and create negative reactions. However, thinking from the viewpoint of adult social development, the teacher might ask: Why don't people participate? Why do certain people monopolize the discussion?

Answers could be that some persons are not interested, some are afraid of being put down, some don't understand the issue, some feel unworthy to voice an opinion. Others are discouraged or worried or ill. One may have a deep need to be in control of something. Another is seeking attention.

You begin to see, then, that the basic problem isn't simply that some don't participate and others monopolize time. Therefore, limiting yourself (and the group) to the lecture method would not be a solution, only a way of avoiding the problems. In most cases, developing a true group gives you a better chance to see the real problems and to find solutions that will help individuals, as well as improve the group session.

Develop Group Consciousness

Let the members see that you think of them and yourself as a group. Let them know what you believe about Christian groups—that the members respect one another, exchange ideas and benefits, and work together to make the group a success.

Usually some formal organization promotes group cohesiveness. Guide the group in working out a simple set of guidelines or group constitution. Have the group select a group historian, who will keep a calendar and a group scrapbook. This person, or a separate group reporter, and perhaps a group photographer can work together to submit material to a local paper, the church bulletin, and newsletters.

As people become more aware of themselves as a group, they are more conscious of how the group perceives them and less likely to ignore the feelings of the group.

> **RATE** How developed is the group consciousness among your members? What are some specific things you or your group does to promote this feeling of togetherness? What can you do to strengthen this?

Establish Group Norms

Encourage the group to share their feelings and concerns. Together make some rules about discussion procedures. For example, ideas must be presented in positive terms, not as contradictions of other persons, and time limits must be observed. Talk about sharing responsibilities, hospitality for newcomers, and obligations of the group in relation to other church personnel and programs.

Many people have never learned how to participate in a group discussion. It is appropriate for the leader to talk openly about methods and rules of good discussions. This is an extra service to the members and to the church, for it prepares adults to participate constructively in other meetings. Frustration and hurt feelings could be avoided in church business meetings, for example, if people were more informed about, and practiced in, open discussion.

> **DELIBERATE**   Lead a discussion of how to participate in a group discussion. You may look up helpful articles and guidelines on the Internet so you have some solid guidelines before throwing the floor open to suggestions and comments from members of the group.

Consider Goals and Purposes

You may find that some adults say they wish to listen and not become involved in small group activities. Yet, they are active in other groups. Often this is because group leaders don't create a feeling of continuity and purpose. You can help change these attitudes by introducing the concept of shared goals and purposes.

Demonstrate and Encourage Leadership

Studies show that teachers, after all their training in methods, are more likely to imitate the teachers they remember than to practice a formally learned methodology. To some extent, every small group is a leadership training school, and every teacher is a model of Christian leadership. As you show skill in guiding group activity, you are teaching the group members how to relate to others and how to exercise Christian leadership at home, at work, and in the various church ministries.

This is especially important for young adults, who are deciding whether to commit themselves in relationships of partnership and service. It is important too for mature adults, who seek effective ways of passing on to others what they have acquired. Even older adults learn from experience in groups, which makes them more competent and comfortable in making adjustments to new situations.

Some Specific Suggestions

Open the group with an invitation to participate, rather than making a presentation and then asking questions. Ask if anyone has a question or an idea or suggestion at the beginning. At the close of the session, express appreciation for those who have participated. Give some suggestions for further study. Mention a question that was not answered and suggest that someone pursue it and report back. Ask a question or mention an objective in relation to the next lesson. Make a few specific assignments and a general appeal to study the lesson.

When someone responds during the discussion, be a good listener. If necessary, help him to restate or clarify his ideas, but never let anyone feel personally put down.

Try to keep the interaction going among the members, not just between you and one member at a time. Have them seek information from one another and answer one another's questions.

Ask for contributions related specifically to the interests, experiences, and accomplishments of the members. Whenever the lesson naturally calls for specialized input, give someone an opportunity to share his knowledge. For example, someone in your group may be familiar with carpentry, farming, baking bread, sewing, weaving, dying cloth, racing, or traveling in the Holy Land. The possibilities for constructive input are almost limitless.

Summary

Rapid social changes have made it necessary for the church to reevaluate its ministry to adults. The purpose of this chapter has been to approach teaching adults from the viewpoint of group interaction, based on a knowledge of their nature and needs at the various stages of social development.

Stages in the life span are defined in terms of critical needs or decision points that characterize the period for most individuals. These critical decisions relate very closely to the development of spiritual life and involvement in the church. Therefore, the informed and sensitive leader plans the group session to meet individual needs and to help each adult become a contributing member of the local church and the body of Christ.

Evaluate Your Understanding

1. What are two objectives of discussing group processes and leadership in the context of leading adults?

2. What is the meaning of the term crisis as it relates to Erickson's three major stages of the adult lifespan?
3. What are Erickson's three stages of adulthood, and what is the crisis associated with each stage?
4. At which stage are the various members of your group? At which stage are you?
5. What is the term for the tension between forming relationships and pulling away from people and social obligations? Describe how this tension plays out in young adulthood.
6. A person will have a foundation for the intimacy and commitment required in mature love if he or she has learned what two things during childhood and adolescence?
7. According to the chapter, what is a clear sign that adulthood has been reached?
8. According to this chapter, what are characteristics of emotionally healthy and mature individuals?
9. The most significant concept of mid-adult life is generativity. What does this term mean?
10. Based on what you have learned in this chapter, compare and contrast an older adult who has developed integrity with one who has not.

Activate

▶ The longer a person is part of a group without speaking, the harder it becomes for him or her to break the silence. Consider non-threatening ways to get everyone talking as soon as possible. Simple ideas include asking each person to tell about his or her holiday plans, share one prayer request, or tell one thing he or she is looking forward to (or dreading) in the coming week.

▶ Plan a group event—picnic, party, sporting event—where adults in the first developmental stage can forge relationships. Be sure each person has some responsibility—something to bring, plan, do, coordinate, or give.

▶ Present a need to your small group in the second stage of adult development and let them come up with ideas—and a plan—for how to meet it.

▶ With your group, brainstorm ways of living life now that will leave a legacy that will outlive them.

▶ Find opportunities for your group members in the third stage of adult development to mentor and influence others who are younger. This works well when matching a senior adult with a young adult—especially one without a godly parental role model. Consider inviting a younger group for a meal, establish a monthly "adoptive grandparent" activity, exchange names and e-mail addresses with members of a younger group for a "pen pal" experience, or volunteer as a group to help with a children's or youth activity. For the safety of both adults and children, never allow one adult to be alone with a child or children.

10

RELATIONSHIPS IN A PLURALISTIC COMMUNITY

*Once you have been reconciled to God,
you have no problem with being reconciled with others.*

FRED LUTER

"THAT'S MY GROUP LEADER—THE FAT ONE."

Several people turned to stare at the speaker. Who would say a thing like that, so loudly, among all these people at the entrance of the church? It was a young woman recently arrived from Central America to attend a local college. She was smiling and waving.

I sure like my group leader, she was thinking, *a nice, round, friendly woman. She's not skinny and impersonal like so many of these North Americans.*

To go and teach all nations seems like a great challenge. But, incredibly, the challenge is even greater when the nations come to you. Most churches have active, productive missions programs. A large majority of workers and members cooperate fully, expressing a kind of pride in being "missionary-minded." But suddenly the "red and yellow and black" of the familiar children's chorus aren't confined to a figure of speech: They're in your group. What once could be accomplished with prayers and offerings now demands face-to-face relationships.

With about a million legal immigrants, plus the uncounted ones, coming into the United States each year, no Christian church can be entirely unaffected. No study of group processes is complete without some attention to cross-cultural and multiethnic factors. In addition to conventional tenets of world missions, two major principles must be acknowledged and considered:

1. Effective Christian ministry requires appreciation and respect for human diversity and the dignity and worth of all persons for whom Christ died.
2. The church is obligated to prepare its members for life and ministry in the pluralistic community that surrounds them and their place of worship.

Small groups meet two distinct needs. One is to see that enlightened Christian hospitality prevails in any local church for any person who desires to worship and fellowship there. The other is to help its members to appreciate one another and enjoy working together as multiethnic groups.

As a leader, you are in a better position than anyone else to provide instruction and leadership as the church meets this modern challenge. The following material will give you the understanding and background you need for the task.

> **EVALUATE**   How well is your group meeting these two needs? How might individuals of another race or ethnic group view your current group? How welcome would they feel?

Concepts of Culture and Ethnicity

Culture may be described as everything human beings invent as they meet their needs and adapt to nature (their own as well as their environment's): what they produce or make to feed, clothe, and house themselves; their patterns of interaction, institutions, and religious and artistic expressions. Every aspect of the environment affects culture. The classic example is that loose pieces of cloth serve as clothing in hot climates, but tailored clothing, which fits cozily to the body, was invented in cold climates. Such a cultural difference has indeed caused people to think and act in diverse ways—as well as to judge another culture on the basis of their own. Which is more practical, a sarong or a suit?

Each person is affected by a set of cultural components. Most social interactions are greatly influenced by these components. In other words, most people are comfortable with those whose cultural components are similar to their own.

Why do you like a person? You may reply that it is because of his or her personality. But think about it as you read the list of cultural components that follows.

- Religion
- Language
- Ethnic background
- Occupational experiences
- Socioeconomic status
- Education
- Tastes in art and music
- Country of birth
- Rural or urban background
- Special experiences (e.g., military service)

> **CONTEMPLATE** In how many of the categories do you and your best friends fit well together?

If you have close friends who differ greatly from you in several of the categories, then you have a good foundation for work with multicultural groups. Otherwise, you may find it helpful to widen the circle of your friends and learn to appreciate the tastes and experiences of others.

One aspect of culture is *ethnicity*. Its principal distinguishing feature speaks of a shared and rather complex set of values, traditions, customs, religions, language, national origin, and perhaps physical features. Also, for those who are deeply committed to their ethnic heritage, ethnicity has an emotional quality, similar to the feeling of belonging to a family. In fact, the foundations of ethnicity are laid in early childhood, as are the foundations of cherished family traditions, concepts of right and wrong, and religion.

The second distinguishing feature of ethnicity is that full commitment to an ethnic identity is more or less voluntary. One of the unique and exceptional freedoms that the United States offers its changing immigrant populations is the freedom to identify with an ethnic group, or to accommodate to the general society.

Unfortunately, it is true that ethnic and racial bias and discrimination still exist in the United States. However progress has been made. Today most Americans can celebrate their ancestry, or they can ignore it. Whether or not they live in an ethnic neighborhood and expose their children to the language and customs of their own roots is, for an increasing number of Americans, optional.

Although there is no agreement on the exact definition of *ethnicity*, it is generally accepted that ethnicity has four major areas of influence. That is, a person's ethnic background may be examined in relation to these four factors.

1. *Communication.* Except for physical features, the most pronounced and obvious distinction among ethnic groups is the language and nonverbal communications patterns. Language not only forms a barrier to understanding between groups, but also determines thought patterns and categories by which one group interprets and evaluates the culture of another. Some groups are more overtly expressive and use more gestures than others. The same gesture may have culturally different meanings, and this can create confusion and misunderstanding.
2. *Ways of learning and reasoning.* North Americans tend to think in terms of logic, science, and competition, with emphasis on verbal skills. Testing almost always involves reading, writing, and speed. It is completely individualistic, so that any sharing

of information is considered cheating. In other cultures, cooperation may be expected, speed may not be an indication of intelligence, and philosophical and intuitive ways of knowing may be favored over formal logic.

3. *Value patterns, tastes, and customs.* Probably the best known among ethnic distinctives are the preferences in food, music, and special ceremonies and celebrations. Other areas in which differences may be great are concepts of time and space, and attitudes toward work and material possessions.

4. *Social relationships.* Great differences exist among ethnic groups in child-rearing practices, kinship terms and relations, manner of address and hospitality, behavior in public, and what people expect of one another in various situations.

> **COLLABORATE**   To help members with different cultures and ethnicities within your group better understand and appreciate each other, ask everyone to consider and share how his or her culture influences him or her in each of the four ways mentioned above. Encourage others to ask questions and clarify what is meant or what it means to the person within society. Challenge everyone to be open, honest, and respectful so that everyone feels valued and welcome in the group.

Some Reasons for Cultural Bias

Identity Factors

From your study of the previous chapters, you are now familiar with the fact that individual identity develops from social contacts. People learn what is expected of them in their surroundings and what to expect from others. Any time these expectations are seriously disrupted, people experience discomfort. This may happen, for example, in the formation of step-families.

In a similar manner, an individual may become unsure of himself when he is with a people whose ways are different from his own. The ego, or identity, seems to be in jeopardy. The way of one's own people (or "my way") seems to be depreciated or rejected. So the individual tends to protect his own feelings by blaming the "different" people. This experience of a missionary in Central America illustrates the concept:

The missionary took a child from an isolated village into the city for a visit. Wishing to do something kind, she bought the child a strawberry ice cream cone. She expected the child to respond with pleasure, perhaps even gratitude. Instead, the child screamed, spit out the ice cream, threw the cone into the dust, and said, "It's hot. It's burning me."

The missionary had tried to express her values (being kind to the child) in her own way (buying an ice cream cone). She did not think to find out if the child had a preference. Happily, this missionary knew that only an ice cream cone had been rejected. But suppose she had not been prepared with previous knowledge and understanding of cultural differences. She might have felt personal offense and rejection. She tried to do something nice and was spit on! She might have said Central American children are rude. Or they are stupid, not knowing cold from hot.

This is a simplified explanation of how identity factors can lead to cultural bias, but it is almost too typical of how many cross-cultural problems develop. If you can keep from feeling personally offended when someone seems to reject your customs, you are in a good position to avoid irrational bias.

> **EVALUATE** What makes you uncomfortable around people who are different from you? Such discomfort may indicate a cultural bias or conflict. Often, such biases are easily overcome when we understand where the other person is coming from—why they do or believe as they do. How can you educate yourself about this other culture?

Meaning Factors

Studies of racial and ethnic bias have seemed to indicate that some Christians have contradictory beliefs. They may say that all persons are equal in the sight of God, but they don't demonstrate this belief in their treatment of minorities of various racial or ethnic groups. One explanation for this seeming contradiction is found in the way meanings are associated with certain words and concepts. If evil is called black and purity is called white, the tendency to devalue darker skin tones may be supported unconsciously.

Even more subtle is the meaning of individual responsibility for one's condition. The doctrine of free will relates to sin and salvation. However, some Christians transfer the idea to other aspects of life, so that those who are disadvantaged are blamed or looked down on. Those who are advantaged (even though they did nothing personally to deserve wealth or position) are given preferential treatment.

The strangest contradiction is that the "missionary attitude" can actually bring about a devaluation of persons. When one knows his religion (or political or philosophical viewpoint) is the correct one and thinks of others only as targets for evangelism, he may feel superior to them.

Belonging Factors

The sense of belonging—Christian community—is one of the essential aspects of Christian groups. A problem arises when this great asset is turned into a liability by "us" and "them" feelings and behaviors. Close identification with a group can sometimes lead people to reject outsiders or be reluctant to open the circle to newcomers. Many evangelical Christians have found refuge in the Christian group, escaping unpleasant associations of a former lifestyle. Their desire to keep the group safe and comfortable for themselves may reinforce a bias against those who are "different."

> **CONTEMPLATE**   Rather than focusing on the ways various ethnic groups are different, consider ways in which they are alike. Come up with a list—individually or in conjunction with group members— of traits, experiences, desires, fears, interests, needs, strengths, and accomplishments that all or most members of the group share in common. Remind yourself of these common bonds often.

Types of Ethnic Relations

Ethnic groups don't automatically have conflicts with one another. In a free society, several types of relationships are possible. The most common follow:

- *Segregation.* The groups share the general culture, but don't interact with one another. A strong dominant group may exist.
- *Pluralism.* The groups maintain definite identities, but work together cooperatively in many ways, without domination of one over the other.
- *Integration.* Individuals may identify to any desired degree with an ethnic group, but emphasis is on a policy of equality in the greater society.
- *Assimilation.* Individuals gradually come to identify more with the general society than with an ethnic segment. This usually happens over several generations.

All types of ethnic relationships are present in the United States today. The term *pluralism* is used most often to express the general multiethnic state of the country. This term is relatively free of emotional connotations and more than any of the others signifies respect for all groups, without trying either to separate them or force them together.

The Small Group in a Multiethnic Society

It Provides a Support Group

As the multiethnic character of the society develops, small group becomes even more important as the agency that prepares candidates for contributing membership in the Body. Everything that has been said about socialization of children and adolescents can be applied in some way to helping individuals of various backgrounds identify and find acceptance through group processes. Everything discussed concerning the need of people to feel safe in seeking information, asking questions, expressing feelings, and contributing

ideas certainly applies here. No other established facility is potentially as well equipped as the small group to meet the needs of multiethnic peoples seeking information and emotional support in a Christian context.

Another unique function of the small group is its ministry to children and youth who are moving from distinct ethnic identification into the mainstream of American society. It is clear from history that many young people eventually leave churches that have exclusively ethnic and non-English ministries. Large numbers of such young people have drifted away entirely.

The modern church is in a strategic position now to see that this does not happen in the future. As you express appreciation for persons of diverse backgrounds and guide your group members to interact comfortably with one another, you are making a place where young people can try out independence without complete rejection of their roots. You are providing a support group for persons in transition, life's most vulnerable stage. You can help them to see God's will about permanent church affiliation and Christian ministry.

It Teaches the Christian World View

The subject of missions has always been included in the church's curriculum because it is essential to the development of Christian thought and practice (or world view). The Christian way of thinking includes a concern for lost souls and a sense of responsibility for people throughout the world. The essential characteristic of this world view is that God created all people. He loves them all and is not willing that any should perish.

As local neighborhoods become populated with those of many ethnic backgrounds, the church must renew its commitment to the Christian world view. It must teach that racial bias of any sort is a rejection of the Great Commission.

A fundamental difference between racism and Christianity makes it absolutely impossible for a true Christian to be racist. The essential meaning of racism is that persons are evaluated on the basis of genetics. A person can't change his race and this biological factor is used to determine his worth. The essential meaning of Christianity is completely opposite: The source of personal worth is not in genes, but in the attitude of the heart in accepting divine grace through Jesus Christ. Accepting divine grace makes all Christians—without exception—of equal value.

The general aim of the group leader is to provide a platform for true integration. That is, each person is encouraged to feel comfortable with his own ethnicity, and yet no less a part of the group. The missions program in the church takes on a new and even greater excitement as persons of many backgrounds join together. As "we" and "they" become one, our group can be a living example of that ideal group, those purchased by Christ from every tribe and language and people and nation to share His love and glory.

> **COLLABORATE**   Consider meeting with a Christian leader of an ethnicity, race, or culture different from your own. Brainstorm ways to work together to overcome racism, bias, and discomfort with people of different backgrounds. Discuss ways to integrate activities and fellowship between the two groups.

Summary

Think again, carefully and prayerfully, of the two major principles of Christian education in a pluralistic society. First, effective Christian ministry requires appreciation and respect for human diversity and the worth of all persons for whom Christ died. Second, the church is obligated to prepare its members for life and ministry in the pluralistic community that surrounds them and their place of worship.

To live and work in accordance with these principles, you need a knowledge of culture, ethnicity, and intercultural relations. This chapter has given you a brief overview of this information and offered some suggestions for applying it in your leadership role.

Cultural bias may develop in the church if people desire to enjoy their own group experiences rather than sharing them with others. On the other hand, ethnic groups don't automatically have conflicts, and the leader is in a strategic position to help group members develop positive relationships among themselves.

Since divine grace makes all Christians of equal value, Christianity and racism are totally incompatible. The teacher can help the group become a living example of the ideal group—the Christian community.

Evaluate Your Understanding

1. Given the growing multi-ethnic and racial nature of today's society, what two major principles does the text say group leaders must acknowledge and consider?
2. As related to the church responsibility in a pluralistic community, what two distinct needs do small groups meet?
3. What is culture?
4. What is the difference between culture and ethnicity?
5. What are four major areas in which a person's ethnicity influences his or her life?
6. Give an example—from your own experience or from this chapter—of cultural bias. How can we avoid problems that can stem from cultural bias?
7. What is the contradiction of the "missionary attitude," and how can we avoid this in dealing with people of different races, ethnicities, and cultures within our small group?
8. How can one of the essential aspects of Christian groups—the sense of belonging to a Christian community—turn into a liability if we are not careful?
9. What are the four types of relationships possible within a multi-ethnic context? Which best describes your group? Your church?
10. Define *pluralism*.

Activate

▶ As an ice breaker or conversation starter, play the "I've Never" game with your group. Each member names one thing he or she has never done, and other members of the group react—asking questions, relating their own experiences, etc. This is a great way to identify and learn to understand differences and similarities between various group members.

▶ Find a way to celebrate and explore the customs, foods, and perspectives of the various ethnic groups represented in your group or in the community from which you'd like to draw group members. What better way to make an unrepresented group feel welcome than to invite them to share with your group and educate them about their background, culture, and customs.

▶ Ask God to give you love, understanding, and compassion for people who are not like you.

▶ Ask God to expand your group to include people of different cultural and ethnic groups.

▶ Strive to make your group a place that welcomes everyone. Encourage group members to be aware of God's love for all people and to consciously accept and welcome people of different ethnic, racial, or cultural backgrounds.

▶ Immerse yourself into different cultures (e.g.,food, entertainment, celebrations, history). Find something you love about each one.

ACKNOWLEDGMENTS

When I wrote *The Dynamic Classroom* in 1987, the culture was very different from what it is today, but the principles of success in leadership were the same. So, when I decided to redo the book, I found two capable and creative editors to help me update and supplement the text.

Sylvia Lee brought the language up to date for the contemporary reader. Tammy Bicket, who developed the ideas for application, is a teacher who knows how to reach the contemporary student. Together, they helped me make *Small Group Dynamics for Dynamic Leaders* a guide for those who teach and lead small groups and train leaders for effective ministry.

Early in my educational experience, I developed the idea that to learn is the best thing you can do for yourself and to teach is the best thing you can do for another person. This book is built upon that idea.

Dr. Billie Davis
October 2017

NOTES

Chapter 1: Jesus and His Disciples: The Model Group
1. From early times it has been thought that he [that is, the disciple of John the Baptist who was with Andrew but is unnamed by the Gospel writers] was the beloved disciple, and, while this is not proven, it may well be the case" (Leon Morris, *The Gospel According to John* [Grand Rapids, Mich.: Eerdmans, 1971], p.155).

2. Barclay, William, The Daily Bible Study Series, vol. 1 (Philadelphia, Pa.: The Westminster Press, 1956).

FOR FURTHER READING   *The Master of Relationships: How Jesus Formed His Team* (Third Edition) by Rick Zachary, Bonhoeffer Publishing 2014

Chapter 2: A Group Is People Sharing
1. Cartwright, D. and Zander, A., *Group Dynamics: Research and Theory,* 3rd ed. (New York: Harper and Row Publishers, 1965).

2. Lewin, Kurt, *Field Theory in Social Science* (New York: Harper Publishers, 1951).

3. Sherif, M.; Harvey, O. J.; White, B. J.; Hood, W. R.; Sherif, C. W., *Intergroup Conflict and Cooperation: The Robber's Cave Experiment* (Norman, Okla.: Institute of Group Relations, 1961).

FOR FURTHER READING   *Small Groups with Purpose: How to Create Healthy Communities* by Steve M. Glades, Baker Books 2011

Chapter 3: A Group Is for Belonging
1. Durkheim, Emile, *The Division of Labor in Society* (Glencoe, Ill.: Free Press, 1947).

2. Schutz, W. C., FIRO: *A Three-Dimensional Theory of Interpersonal Behavior* (New York: Rinehart and Co., Inc., 1958).

3. Schachter, S., *The Psychology of Affiliation* (Palo Alto, Calif.: Stanford University Press, 1959).

4. Burns, Robert, "To a Louse," *The Best Loved Poems of the American People* (New York: Garden City Publishing Co., 1936).

FOR FURTHER READING *The Church and the Crisis of Community: A Practical Theology of Small-Group Ministry* by Theresa F. Latini, Eerdmans 2011

Chapter 4: How People Act in Groups

1. Tuckman, B. W., "Development Sequences in Small Groups," *Psychological Bulletin*, 63 (1965):384–399.

2. Sherif, M., *The Psychology of Social Norms* (New York: Harper and Row Publishers, 1936).

FOR FURTHER READING *Making Small Groups Work: What Every Small Group Leader Needs to Know* (Abridged Edition) by Henry Cloud and John Townsend, Zondervan 2003

Chapter 5: Understanding and Misunderstanding

1. Schramm, Wilbur, ed., *Communications in Modern Society* (Urbana, Ill.: The University of Illinois Press, 1948).

FOR FURTHER READING *Field Guide for Small Group Leaders: Setting the Tone, Accommodating Learning Styles, and More* by Sam O'Neal, IVP Connect 2012

Chapter 6: The Leadership Role in Teaching

1. McGregor, Douglas, *The Human Side of Enterprise* (New York: McGraw-Hill, 1960).

2. Lewin, K; Lippit, R.; and White, R., "Patterns of Aggressive Behavior in Experimentally Created Social Climates," *Journal of Social Psychology* 10 (1939): 271–299.

3. Berne, Eric, *Transactional Analysis* (New York: Grove Press, 1961).

4. Harris, Thomas A., *I'm OK—You're OK: A Practical Guide to Transactional Analysis* (New York: Harper and Row Publishers, 1969).

FOR FURTHER READING *Small Group Success: Changing Lives One Group at a Time* by Bradley D. Wright, Silver Leaf Publishers 2015

Chapter 7: Children Learn and Grow in Groups
1. Erikson, Erik H., *Childhood and Society*, 2nd ed. (New York: Norton, 1964).

FOR FURTHER READING   *Children's Ministry in the Way of Jesus* by David Csinos and Ivy Beckwith, IVP Books 2013

Chapter 8: Adolescence Can Be Defined as Relationships
1. Erikson, Erik H., *Childhood and Society*, 2nd ed. (New York: Norton, 1964).

FOR FURTHER READING   *Growing Young: Six Essential Strategies to Help Young People Discover and Love Your Church* by Kara Powell and Jake Mulder, Baker Books 2016

Chapter 9: Mature Christians Work Together
1. Erikson, Erik H., *Childhood and Society*, 2nd ed. (New York: Norton, 1964).

FOR FURTHER READING   *Shaping the Journey of Emerging Adults: Life-Giving Rhythms for Spiritual Transformation* by Richard R. Dunn and Jana L. Sundene IVP Books 2012

Chapter 10: Relationships in a Pluralistic Community

FOR FURTHER READING   *Ministering Cross-Culturally: A Model for Effective Personal Relationships* by Sherwood G. Lingenfelter and Marvin K. Mayers Baker Books (Academic) 2016

BIBLIOGRAPHY

Boren, M. Scott, *Leading Small Groups in the Way of Jesus*. Westmont, Ill.: IVP, 2015

Brown, Gregory, *Equipping Small Group Leaders: A Concise Church Leadership Training*. CreateSpace Independent Publishing Platform, 2017

Comiskey, Joel, *2000 Years of Small Groups: A History of Cell Ministry in the Church*. Lima, Ohio: CCS Publishing, 2014

Donahue, Bill, Russ G. Robinson, *Building a Life-Changing Small Group Ministry: A Strategic Guide for Leading Group Life in Your Church*. Grand Rapids: Zondervan, 2012

Egli, Jim, Dwight Marble, Small Groups, *Big Impact: Connecting People to God and One Another in Thriving Groups*. Kindle format, 2014

Frazee, Randy, *The Connecting Church 2.0: Beyond Small Groups to Authentic Community*. Grand Rapids: Zondervan, 2013

House, Brad, *Community: Taking Your Small Group Off Life Support*. Wheaton: Crossway, 2011

Joiner, Reggie, Tom Shefchunas, *Lead Small: Five Big Ideas Every Small Group Leader Needs to Know*. Cumming, Georgia: Orange Books, 2012

Stetzer, Ed, Eric Geiger, *Transformational Groups: Creating a New Scorecard for Groups*. Nashville: B & H Books, 2014

Surratt, Chris, *Small Groups for the Rest of Us: How to Design Your Small Group System to Reach the Fringes*. Nashville: Thomas Nelson, 2015

www.smallgroups.com
www.groupsmatter.com

CPSIA information can be obtained
at www.ICGtesting.com
Printed in the USA
LVHW082356310120
645532LV00008B/21